D0393228

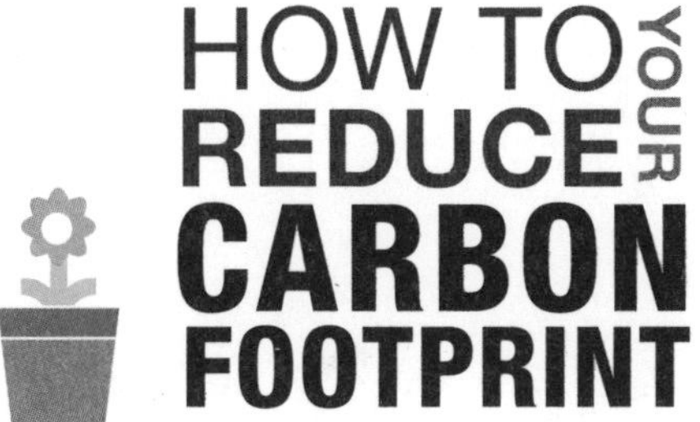
HOW TO
REDUCE
YOUR
CARBON
FOOTPRINT

HOW TO REDUCE YOUR CARBON FOOTPRINT

365 SIMPLE WAYS TO SAVE ENERGY, RESOURCES, AND MONEY

JOANNA YARROW

CHRONICLE BOOKS
SAN FRANCISCO

How to Reduce Your Carbon Footprint
Joanna Yarrow

First published in the United States in 2008 by Chronicle Books LLC.
First published in the United Kingdom and Ireland in 2008 by Duncan Baird Publishers.

Library of Congress Cataloging-in-Publication Data available.

ISBN: 978-0-8118-6393-3

Manufactured in Spain

Conceived, created, and designed by Duncan Baird Publishers.

Duncan Baird Publishers Ltd
Sixth Floor
Castle House
75–76 Wells Street
London W1T 3QH

Editor: James Hodgson
Designer: Luana Gobbo
Managing Designer: Suzanne Tuhrim
Managing Editor: Christopher Westhorp
Commissioned Artwork: Peter Grundy

Typeset in Helvetica Neue

10 9 8 7 6 5 4 3 2 1

Chronicle Books LLC
680 Second Street
San Francisco, California 94107

www.chroniclebooks.com

This book is printed using vegetable-based inks on FSC-certified paper.

As there is no single standardized approach to calculating carbon footprints, the basis of calculations may vary slightly between figures.

CONTENTS

KEY TO SYMBOLS

Behavior change
Purchasing decision
Long-term payback
Short-term payback
D.I.Y.
Specialist needed
Major change

INTRODUCTION

Until very recently, most people had never heard of a "carbon footprint." Now, all of a sudden, the phrase is hard to avoid. In an age of slick slogans, fast fashions, and fickle fads it's easy to assume that this is just another quirky passing gimmick. But it could well be the most important concept of our time.

A carbon footprint is the amount of carbon dioxide (CO_2) emitted as a direct or indirect result of an activity. Almost everything we do results in CO_2 emissions—from breathing to traveling, warming our homes to buying food. The illustration opposite gives just a taste of the diverse activities that affect our footprint.

The term "carbon footprint" is relatively new, but the principles behind it are not—human and other forms of life impacting on the environment by emitting carbon dioxide is a pattern as old as the hills; life itself has always depended on and affected the planet's carbon cycle. All organic matter contains carbon, and this is released and reabsorbed in a continuous flow. What's new is the scale of the impact humans are having, and the imbalance it's causing in the biosphere.

WHAT'S THE PROBLEM?

"Greenhouse gases," such as carbon dioxide, in the atmosphere aren't a problem *per se*. In fact they're a good thing—they act like a blanket, helping to trap the sun's heat; and without them the planet would be too cold for life as we know it. Problems occur when they're released into the atmosphere faster than they can be reabsorbed by natural processes.

Since the Industrial Revolution, human activity—primarily through the burning of fossil fuels (coal, oil, and gas)—has been releasing CO_2 that was absorbed over millions of years at a rate far faster than it can be reabsorbed, and it's building up in the atmosphere. At the moment, **CO_2 is being released about three times faster than it can be reabsorbed. Every second, human activity emits another 770 tons—enough to fill 140 Olympic-size swimming pools**.

Concentrations of greenhouse gases are now higher than at any point in the past 800,000 years, and are set to increase by 2.5% each year. While a minority of scientists still quibble about details, the vast majority worldwide agree that climate change resulting from carbon emissions released through human activity is happening, and happening much faster than most predicted.

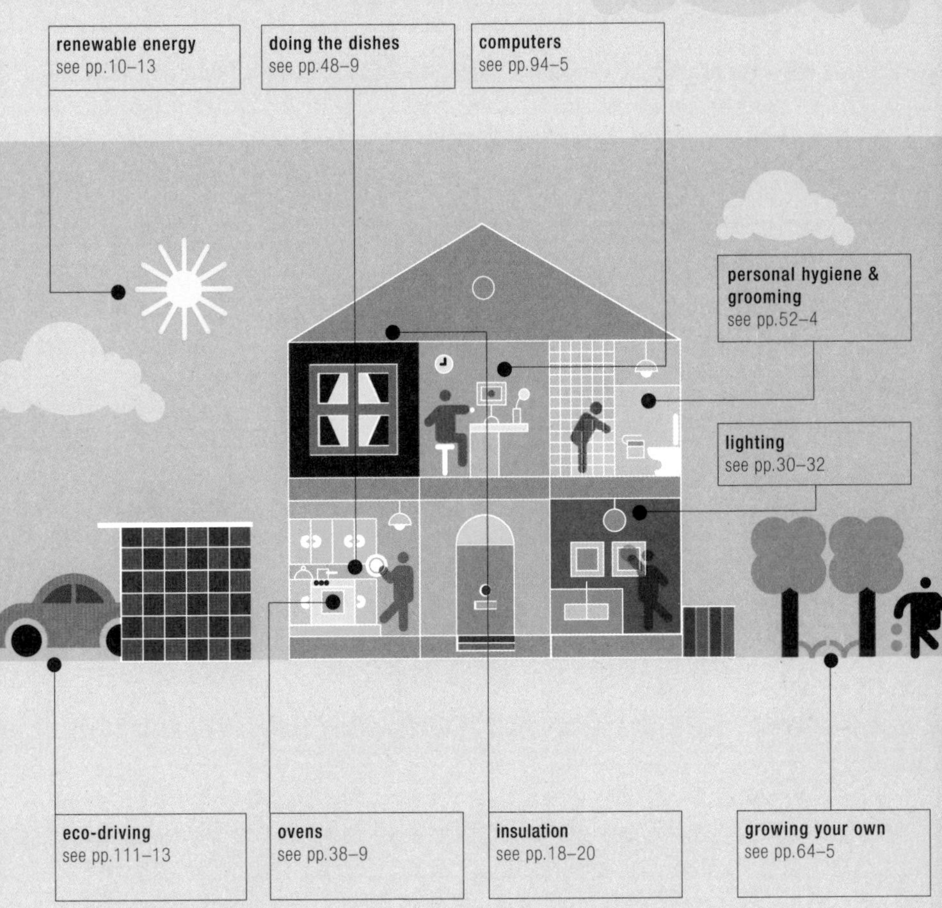
renewable energy
see pp.10–13
doing the dishes
see pp.48–9
computers
see pp.94–5
personal hygiene & grooming
see pp.52–4
lighting
see pp.30–32
eco-driving
see pp.111–13
ovens
see pp.38–9
insulation
see pp.18–20
growing your own
see pp.64–5

In its Fourth Report, published in 2007, the Intergovernmental Panel on Climate Change (IPCC), which brings together the world's top climate scientists, estimated that by 2100 global warming will be in the range of 4.5 to 11.5°F. This would result in the warmest period on Earth for at least 100,000 years.

The problems that these higher temperatures will bring are already beginning to affect us. Unpredictable and extreme weather patterns, rising tides, the destruction of ice shelves, drought, failing crops, and mass movement of climate-change refugees are already hitting the headlines, giving us a small taste of the realities to come unless we take drastic action to change the trajectory we've put the planet on.

WHO'S TO BLAME?

People all over the world are emitting CO_2 at unsustainable rates. But some of us are worse than others. The average European emits around 11 tons per year, while the average American emits over 22 tons—more than 5 times the world average (4 tons). In contrast, in sub-Saharan Africa the average footprint is less than 0.8 tons per person.

Nearly every aspect of our daily lives contributes to our carbon footprint—from heating and lighting our homes and workplaces and powering the appliances we use in them to traveling between them. Less obviously, but equally significantly, the production, processing, transportation, and disposal of the goods and services we use all add to our footprint.

WHAT CAN WE DO ABOUT IT?

We can't, and don't need to, cut our carbon emissions to zero, but we do need to cut back very significantly very quickly to avert much of the predicted chaos. Calculations that look at the Earth's population and the planet's ability to reabsorb CO_2 suggest that the carbon cycle could be brought back under control if we each had a carbon footprint of about 1.7 tons. That's good news if you're living in sub-Saharan Africa, where this would be double most people's carbon budgets, but for most of us this means substantial cuts.

The fact that almost every area of human activity contributes to our carbon footprint might sound like an overwhelming problem. But the good news is that this gives us scope to reduce our footprint in almost every aspect of our lives.

Governments worldwide are debating how best to regulate emissions, and businesses are beginning to take responsibility. But the issues are so enormous, the timescale so pressing, and the potential consequences of inaction so dire that change at every level is crucial.

As individuals, there are numerous things we can each do to reduce our own carbon footprints—in our everyday actions and in our wider sphere of influence as consumers, voters, and global citizens. We all have the power to significantly reduce our footprint by making low-carbon choices.

WHAT ABOUT OFFSETTING?

The idea of "offsetting" our carbon emissions by avoiding the release of, or removing from the atmosphere, an equivalent amount of greenhouse gas somewhere else is becoming increasingly popular.

A growing number of organizations are offering services that claim to do this through funding energy-efficiency projects (e.g. fitting low-energy lightbulbs), low-carbon energy projects and development (e.g. wind farms), and reforestation projects.

Offsetting may appear to be an attractive, pain-free way to reduce your carbon footprint. But by itself this option really is too good to be true. The conventional method of planting trees to offset emissions has a number of flaws—not least the limited space available (**the U.S. would need to plant 30 billion trees a year to absorb the CO_2 it emits!**). And other offsetting methods rely on timescales that we simply can't afford—a flight's emissions happen immediately, whereas a low-carbon project may avoid the same emissions only over a long period of time, with those emissions from the plane still having an effect in the atmosphere.

We can't avoid the urgent need to minimize our carbon footprint, and this should be prioritized. But "offsetting" any unavoidable emissions by investing in low-carbon projects, speeding the transition to low-carbon ways of living, and encouraging businesses to do the same through carbon markets can be useful.

ABOUT THIS BOOK

This book doesn't lay down a set of rules that everyone should adhere to in order to reduce their carbon footprint. Everyone's lifestyle and interests are different, and in my experience over-prescriptive diets often trigger a rebellion after a short while! Instead, it outlines how everyday life contributes to our carbon footprint and suggests a number of actions that could help trim it.

I hope that this book will help you to adjust your lifestyle to reduce your footprint—while enhancing your quality of life along the way.

Joanna Yarrow, Beyond Green
(www.beyondgreen.co.uk)

On March 19, 2007, **wind power** briefly became the single biggest provider of electricity in Spain, accounting for **27%** of total production.
Every **2 minutes** the sun gives the Earth more energy than we use in **a year**.
In 2005, **hydropower** accounted for **63%** of renewable energy produced worldwide.
There are more than a million **geothermal heat exchange** systems currently operating in the U.S. Their positive impact equates to taking **1.3 million cars** off the road; or planting **400 million trees**; or reducing annual fuel consumption by **21.5 million barrels of crude oil**.

RENEWABLE ENERGY

However much you streamline your energy use, you're still going to need *some* power. By taking advantage of the growing availability of renewable energy, you'll keep the carbon footprint of your energy use as low as possible.

  **SUN SPOTS** Photovoltaic (PV) technology harnesses energy from the sun's rays to create electricity. Modern PV panels require only daylight (not necessarily direct sunlight) to generate electricity and so can still generate some power on a cloudy day. Prices are falling rapidly—in fact, it's predicted that solar power will cost around the same as coal-fired power by 2010. Installing photovoltaic panels on your roof or walls will provide free electricity to power your home. If that's too much of an investment, **try out one of the many pieces of solar equipment**—from cellphone chargers to radios—now on the market. You may never need to buy another battery.

  **WINDS OF CHANGE** The price of wind power has dropped by about 90% over the last two decades,

WHY DO WE NEED RENEWABLE ENERGY?

By 2030, global energy use is projected to be at least double what it is today. The International Energy Agency predicts that 80% of this new growth will be met by fossil fuels—coal, oil, and gas. If this trend continues unchecked, it will result in a catastrophic **52% rise in greenhouse gas emissions** around the world.

Meanwhile, as supplies of fossil fuels become scarcer, energy bills will rocket, and supplies are likely to become a growing source of political tension.

Renewable energy sources are an increasingly viable alternative. Not only are they carbon neutral (emitting negligible CO_2 into the atmosphere), they have numerous other advantages. They rely on free fuel, so running costs are low and predictable, avoiding the economic

and in some areas the technology's booming. For example, in northern Germany wind provides more than 20% of the power used, and installed generating capacity has been growing by around 28% per year. You could use a small turbine to charge a battery system in your home, which could cut your electricity bill by a third and your household carbon footprint by up to half a ton of CO_2 a year. If you produce an excess, you could sell it to your local utility. Or you could **opt for a green pricing program** (see opposite), in which you support a utility's investment in renewable energy by paying a premium on your bill.

TAKE TO THE WAVES The energy held in the oceans' waves, currents, tides, and temperature differentials can be tapped for human use. Most of the technologies in these areas are still at the experimental stage, but several significant and successful tidal-power installations are already in action. Australia, Portugal, and Scotland are among a growing list of countries investing in ocean-energy technologies—Scotland is expected to have the world's largest wave farm up and running by 2008, able to supply power to 2,000 homes. Find out more, and if you're

chaos of fuel price fluctuations. They're abundantly available worldwide, and are far less vulnerable to terrorist attack than conventional energy sources.

Renewable resources currently supply only a small share of global energy production, but wind and solar power are the fastest-growing energy sources in the world. The costs of these and other renewables are falling rapidly as technologies develop, production becomes increasingly automated, and economies of scale are achieved.

If progress in this sector continues at current rates, **up to a billion people could use renewable energy in the next decade**, and renewables could account for a third to a half of global energy production by 2050.

in favor of this carbon-neutral power source, **support any proposals for installations in your local area.**

GO TO GROUND The ground absorbs and stores heat from the sun. Geothermal heat exchange involves embedding a network of pipes beneath the ground to harness this natural warmth, which can then be used to heat, or—in a reverse process—to cool, buildings. (See p.22.)

POWER PLANTS Biomass produced from organic materials, either directly from plants or indirectly from industrial or agricultural by-products, has huge potential as a renewable energy source. For example, it can be used to heat your home (see pp.21–2) or as a motor fuel (see pp.118–19), although there are limitations to the land available to grow virgin crops.

DAM IT At present, the most widespread form of renewable energy is hydropower. However, in the developed world most appropriate sites have already been exploited, so it's likely that before too long this will be overtaken by faster-growing sectors, such as wind and solar power.

SIGN UP FOR GREEN POWER

Even if you can't generate your own energy at home, you may still be able to meet your household's electricity needs using renewable power by signing up to one of the growing number of companies supplying energy from renewable sources. Green pricing programs are now available to more than 50% of U.S. electricity customers. If your current supplier doesn't offer a green power product, and your home state allows retail electricity competition, look for an alternative supplier that does provide green pricing.

Fossil fuels are being depleted **100,000 times** faster than they are formed.

SUN AND SHADE

Instead of relying entirely on mechanical heating and cooling, use sun exposure and shading to keep your home at a comfortable temperature.

TRAIN VINES UP TRELLISES on the hottest side of the house. Keep the trellis at least 6 in. from the wall to provide a buffer of cool air.

PLANT TREES to provide summer shade and block winter winds. If you go for deciduous trees, they will provide the additional benefit of letting the sun through in winter.

FIT AWNINGS or movable roof overhangs to block out hot summer sun, but allow it in during the winter. Light-colored draperies and shades can also help reduce heat gain. In winter, keep them open during the day to let sunlight in.

PAINT YOUR HOME a light color if you live in a warm climate, or a dark color if your winters are long and cold. Special reflective, or absorbent, roof coatings are also available.

WORK WITH THE SUN

Traditionally, buildings were designed to take advantage of their local surroundings and climate. Thick walls would keep the summer heat out and retain warmth in the winter. **In hot climates**, buildings were painted light colors to reflect the sun's heat. Windows were relatively small to keep out the sun, and shady, leafy courtyards helped keep the interior cool. **In cold climates**, buildings were painted dark colors to absorb the sun's heat, and south-facing windows were larger to take advantage of the sun's warmth.

With the advent of central heating and air-conditioning, the principles of passive heating and cooling were often sidelined, but now many modern architects are returning to this timeless wisdom.

Your house doesn't need to be facing due south to enjoy **passive solar heat gain**. Buildings facing within **30° of due south** still get **90% of the sun's benefit**.

Another way to use plants to minimize heat gain is to plant a **"green roof"** (see p.67). A green roof can reduce a building's heating and cooling costs by up to 50%.

Shading can reduce indoor temperatures by as much as **20°F**, minimizing the need for mechanical cooling.

As much as **half the energy used** in homes and in commercial buildings **goes into heating and cooling**.

In the sun, **black surfaces** can be up to **70°F hotter than white or silver** ones

Dark-colored exteriors absorb **70% to 90%** of the radiant **solar energy** striking a building.

Studies have found that **improving the air-tightness** of dwellings can yield energy savings of **15% to 30%**.

Installing **glass doors around a fireplace** will improve the heat efficiency of the fire and reduce heat loss up the chimney when the fire's not burning.

Draft-proofing the average home effectively can cut its annual CO_2 emissions by around **300–350 lb.**

Besides preventing warm air from escaping during winter, draft-proofing can **stop hot air from coming in** during summer, reducing your need for A/C.

When fitting draft-proofing, allow adequate **ventilation**, especially if you have a wood-burning stove.

DRAFTS

Sitting in a draft isn't just uncomfortable, it's incredibly wasteful—20% of the heat lost from the average home seeps out through unsealed gaps.

DO A HOME DRAFT AUDIT Hold a lit candle next to window and door frames (ideally on a windy day). Wherever it flickers, there's a draft that needs to be plugged.

EXCLUDE DRAFTS Stop heat from sneaking out and make your home more comfortable by applying draft-proofing, or leak-sealing, materials (see right) around doors, windows, and mail slots. **Fill gaps between baseboards and floor** with silicone sealant or quarter-round molding.

KEEP DOORS CLOSED when the heating's on to stop drafts from running through the house.

PLUG YOUR CHIMNEY with a "chimney balloon." This device sits about a foot above the fireplace, and stops warm air from escaping up the flue. Just remember to remove it when you light a fire!

THE INS AND OUTS OF DRAFT-PROOFING

Draft-proofing is an easy, cost-effective way to stop unwanted airflows into and out of your house and reduce your heating (or cooling) bills. There are several main types of material used for this purpose—most are available from home centers:

- **caulk**—made typically of acrylic latex, butyl rubber, or silicone, this is applied with a caulk gun to fill cracks around the edges of window and door frames
- **rope caulk**—this provides a temporary seal around doors and windows during cold weather
- **weatherstripping**—this may consist of a self-adhesive foam strip or other material and, depending on the type, may be applied to the inside of the door/window frame or to the door/window itself
- **door sweep**—a vinyl or aluminum strip attached to the lower edge of a door.

INSULATION

Although it may not turn as many heads as a solar panel or wind turbine, installing good insulation is one of the most significant things you can do to reduce your home's carbon footprint.

  **INSULATE YOUR ATTIC** to avoid losing up to a third of your heating through the roof. In a cold climate, make sure the insulation's at least 11 in. thick to get good results. This traps heat rising from below, prevents the sun baking your home in the summer, and could cut your home's annual CO_2 emissions by up to 1½ tons.

 **LOOK FOR A HIGH R-VALUE** when shopping for insulating material. This is a measure of its thermal resistance—the greater the R-value, the more effective it'll be at resisting heat flow into the building in summer and out of it in winter.

  **REPLACE OLD WINDOWS WITH DOUBLE-GLAZING** to cut the average home's heat loss by up to 20% and to reduce CO_2 emissions by about 1,500 lb. every year. Alternatively, **try "low-**

WHAT'S THE POINT OF INSULATION?

Good insulation keeps heat in during the winter and out during the summer, reducing the need for energy-intensive heating and cooling. Around half of the heat lost from a typical home escapes through the walls and attic, so insulating these areas is a priority. Floor insulation, double-glazing, draft-proofing (see pp.16–17), and tank and pipe insulation (see pp.21–2) also play important roles in regulating your home's temperature. Besides making your home more efficient to run, insulation also provides less obvious benefits, keeping noise out (or in) and helping to prevent mold forming on walls and ceilings (condensation being caused, in part, by fluctuations in temperature). **Find out more about insulation and other energy-saving strategies from Energy Star** (a U.S. government energy-efficiency program).

✓

A typical pound of insulation saves **twelve times** as much energy in its first year in place as the energy used to produce it.

✓

Uninsulated **draperies** can **cut heat loss** through windows by a third, and insulated draperies can reduce it by half.

✓

Natural insulating materials require up to **10 times less energy** to produce than synthetic materials such as fiberglass.

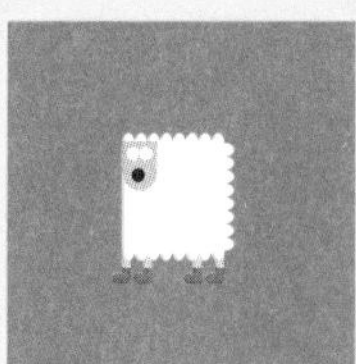

If all residential windows in the U.S. were replaced with Energy Star models, consumers would save a total of **$7 billion** in energy costs in the next 15 years.

Insulating under your first floor could cut your home's heat loss by up to **25%**.

Besides being an excellent insulator, **sheep's wool removes pollutants** such as formaldehyde from the air.

✓

E" (low-emissivity) glass, which allows the same amount of visible sunlight to pass through the window as normal glass but has a special transparent coating that restricts the conduction of thermal energy. This minimizes heat loss during cold weather and heat gain during hot weather. If you're on a budget, **opt for storm windows**, which are a less permanent, but reasonably effective, alternative to new windows, or **apply an adhesive insulating film** to the glass in the fall and peel it off in spring.

CLOSE DRAPERIES, SHADES, OR BLINDS each evening. This can be as effective at keeping warmth in as fitting storm windows—particularly if your draperies are lined.

INSULATE UNDER YOUR FLOOR, and seal gaps between floorboards if they are uncovered.

GET HELP You may be able to get a federal income tax rebate for installing insulation.

DO WHAT COMES NATURALLY Use insulating products derived from natural or recycled materials, such as newspaper, wool, or hemp.

VERTICAL HOLD

Up to 40% of the heat lost from an uninsulated home escapes through the exterior walls. The best way to approach insulating exterior walls depends on whether they are of cavity or solid construction:

- To insulate **cavity walls**, specialist contractors drill a small hole into the wall, through which they inject insulating material, called loose-fill insulation, to fill the cavity. This reduces heat loss through the wall by up to 60%, and could cut the average home's CO_2 emissions by a ton every year.
- To insulate **solid walls**, you have a choice of various materials. The most commonly used type, called batt and roll, or blanket insulation, consists of flexible fibers, typically fiberglass, and comes in several widths, designed to fit between wall studs. Another kind is foam board insulation, which consists of a rigid material, such as expanded polystyrene. This type of insulation reduces the loss of heat through structural elements, but needs to be installed by a professional.

FURNACE

Heating space and water accounts for a significant proportion of our homes' energy requirements. The type of furnace or boiler you have and the way you use it will play a key role in reducing your home's carbon footprint.

  **ALL PART OF THE SERVICE** Get the most out of your furnace by having it serviced annually. If it's more than 10 years old, it's almost certainly pretty inefficient, and ready for an upgrade.

 **GET A CONDENSING FURNACE OR BOILER** When it's time to replace your furnace or boiler, be aware that gas condensing models are much more efficient than conventional ones. They use a heat exchanger to recycle some of the heat in the flue gases, which would otherwise be lost. Such furnaces/boilers are about 90% efficient (compared with 60–70% for a conventional 1980s model).

 **INSULATE YOUR WATER HEATER AND PIPES** If you've got an old water heater, insulate it with a specially designed blanket and cut your CO_2

RENEWABLE HEAT SOURCES

Even the most efficient oil- or gas-fired furnace/boiler will emit a significant amount of CO_2. Heating systems that are powered by renewable energy sources offer a low- or no-carbon alternative.

- **Solar water-heating systems** capture the sun's energy shining onto south-facing collector panels. Depending on the climate you live in, this type of system could meet a large proportion of your hot-water needs.
- Biomass-powered **Combined Heat and Power (CHP) systems** (also called cogeneration) involve burning waste wood chips or other biomass fuel at a neighborhood plant to generate electricity. The heat produced is distributed to local homes to provide heating and hot water. This combined process almost doubles the efficiency of energy use.

emissions by up to 850 lb. a year. New heaters have insulation built in, but it's worth insulating the pipes, using one of the kits available.

KEEP HEAT LOCAL If you're installing a new water heater, situate it close to where the hot water will be used most often to avoid heat loss on long journeys around the house.

INSTALL A DEMAND WATER HEATER This kind of water heater burns energy only when you actually need hot water. It cuts out standby heat loss (up to 4% per hour) and can halve the cost of heating water.

GO IT ALONE If you're not lucky enough to live in an area with a neighborhood CHP system (see p.21), you could invest in a gas-powered domestic model. Although these require fossil fuel, they can reduce energy use by up to 25%.

TURN TO THE SUN If you live in an area of seasonal sun (such as the northern United States), a solar water-heating system should provide all your hot water over the summer and about a third of your needs the rest of the year.

- As long as the fuel comes from a well-managed forest, **wood-burning stoves** are a renewable and carbon-neutral energy source. Traditional fireplaces have been used throughout history to heat buildings, but are generally only 10–30% efficient. Modern stoves can offer up to 85% efficiency. They use wood offcuts, pellets made from compacted sawdust, wood chips, bark, agricultural crop waste, waste paper or other organic materials.
- **Ground-source geothermal heat pumps** harness the heat from beneath your feet. They work by running fluid through a network of collector pipes buried in the ground. The fluid absorbs the earth's natural warmth, which is then converted into superheated gas to warm your home. Geothermal systems can also work in reverse to cool your home in the summer months.

Installing a solar water heater could cut your water-heating bills by **up to 80%**.

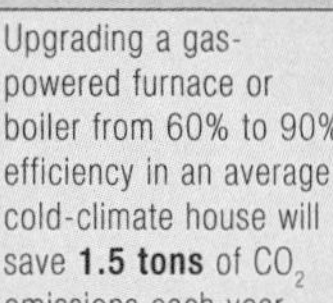

Upgrading a gas-powered furnace or boiler from 60% to 90% efficiency in an average cold-climate house will save **1.5 tons** of CO_2 emissions each year.

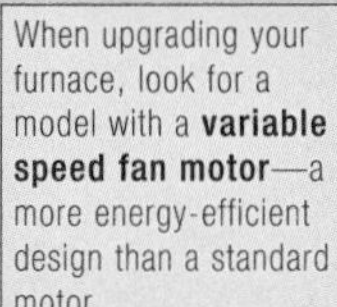

When upgrading your furnace, look for a model with a **variable speed fan motor**—a more energy-efficient design than a standard motor.

In the U.S., almost **80% of furnaces or boilers are close to 30 years old** and ready for an upgrade.

Geothermal heat pumps are 300% efficient: for every unit of electricity required for the pump, they provide 3 units of heat.

The average domestic **solar water-heating system** reduces CO_2 emissions by around **1,100 lb.** per year.

In Western countries, **central heating accounts for up to 60% of CO_2** emissions from homes.

Replace your oil or gas furnace with a carbon-neutral **biomass-powered furnace** and save up to **7 tons** of CO_2 emissions per year.

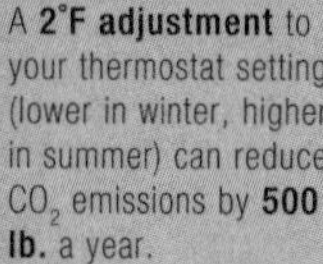

A **2°F adjustment** to your thermostat setting (lower in winter, higher in summer) can reduce CO_2 emissions by **500 lb.** a year.

Typically, **42%** of an American household's energy bill is spent on keeping the home at a comfortable temperature.

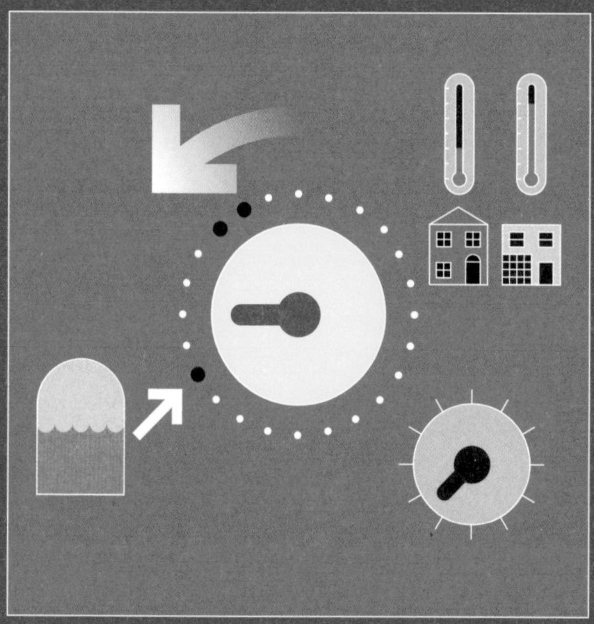

A temperature of **68°F** is considered comfortable for the daytime, but try reducing this, maybe to **65°F**, especially if you're moving around or wearing warm clothes.

Turning the heating off **half an hour before bedtime** should cut your heating bill by about **5%**—and you probably won't notice any drop off in temperature.

HEATING & COOLING CONTROLS

Heating and cooling controls are often tucked out of sight, but they can play a major role in reducing the amount of carbon your home generates.

LOCATE YOUR THERMOSTAT WISELY Make sure that it's on an internal wall in one of the main living areas in your home, so that it can accurately sense the ambient temperature. If it's too close to a heat source, such as a television or lamp, it will overestimate the temperature. Conversely, if it's in a chilly utility room, it will underestimate the temperature, making your furnace work overtime.

HEAT AS YOU GO Heat or cool only the rooms you're using, regulating each room separately with a zone control system.

DON'T SCALD YOURSELF IN THE SHOWER Check your water-heater thermostat and lower it to 120°F if it's at a higher setting. Any hotter than that and you'll only have to mix in cold water to make the temperature bearable.

BUTTONS AND DIALS

Used in a savvy way, the right kind of controls can cut your home heating and cooling costs by up to 25%, so they're worth getting right. You'll need the following:

- a **programmable, or setback, thermostat**, which allows you to set different temperatures for different times (particularly useful if your home is usually unoccupied during the day) and turn your water heater on and off automatically
- a **water-heater thermostat**, which is located on the tank itself—on electric water heaters there is often a thermostat on both of the heating elements.

For maximum efficiency, install a **zone control system**. This enables you to cool or heat different areas of the house at different times and can cut energy consumption by up to 25%.

HEATING OUTLETS

Your heating system will almost certainly be generating a significant proportion of your home's carbon footprint. Make sure you're getting the most out of it by using your registers or radiators effectively.

 **DON'T HIDE YOUR HEAT** Radiators and other heaters need space around them to create a current of warm air, so don't place furniture or heavy draperies in front of them; otherwise you'll end up with warm furnishings and cold rooms.

 **SEAL YOUR HEATING DUCTS** If you've got forced-air heating and cooling, make sure that the ducts leading to registers don't have leaks. Various ways of sealing leaks, including aerosols, are available. This measure could save up to 30% in energy, and as much as $300, a year off your utility bills. Make sure to employ a contractor approved by your state's department of energy.

  **BLEED A RADIATOR** regularly to expel trapped air. This will help to keep it working at maximum efficiency.

HEAT WHERE YOU WANT IT

To get the most out of a radiator's hard work, fit a reflective panel onto the wall behind it (particularly if it's an exterior wall). This ensures that the heat is reflected back into the room instead of soaking into the wall. Radiator panels made from aluminum foil laminates or aluminized plastic films are cheap and easy to install, or you can make your own using a piece of cardboard covered in aluminum foil.

Fit shallow shelving about 2 in. above a radiator to guide heat into the room.

Fitting **reflective panels** behind radiators could **cut** your home's CO_2 **emissions** by up to **400 lb.** a year.

Moving a large piece of **furniture away** from a radiator could **increase** the radiator's **efficiency** by up to **20%**.

Radiators near the top of multistory buildings may **need to be bled more often** than most, as hot air tends to rise through the heating system.

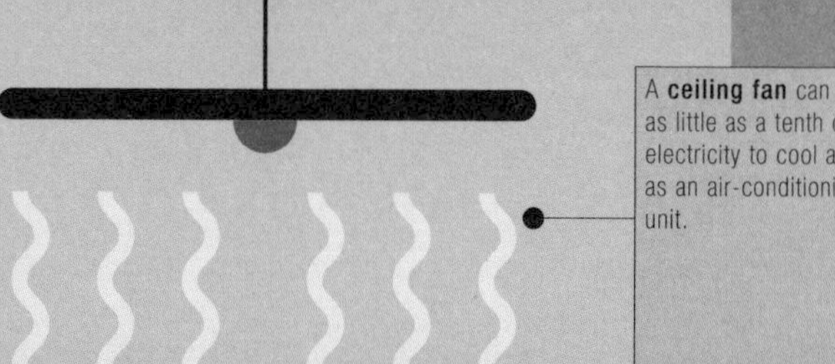

✓

A **ceiling fan** can use as little as a tenth of the electricity to cool a room as an air-conditioning unit.

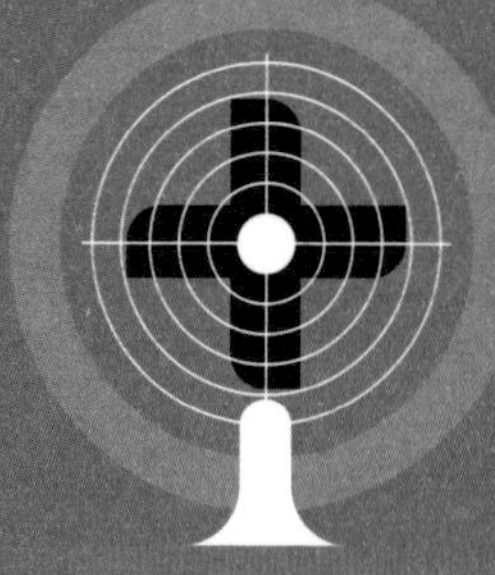

✓

Using water from Lake Ontario to cool its downtown city buildings, the Canadian city of **Toronto** has reduced its annual CO_2 emissions by **79,000 tons**.

✓

Regularly cleaning the filters in your home air-conditioning system can cut its energy use by **5%**, reducing CO_2 emissions by around 250 lb. a year.

✓

Houses that don't have air-conditioning typically use about **half as much energy** as those that do.

!

Air-conditioning uses up to a sixth of the electricity in the U.S., and on hot summer days consumes 43% of the U.S. peak power load.

AIR-CONDITIONING

Mechanical air chilling has a heavy environmental cost. As temperatures rise, low-carbon alternatives will be key to comfortable 21st-century living.

GO BACK TO BASICS Before installing any form of air-cooling system, **improve your insulation** (see pages 18–20) and **draft-proofing** (see pages 16–17) and look for ways to **provide natural shading** (see pages 14–15). These measures can often keep buildings cool without any need for mechanical intervention.

ENCOURAGE A NATURAL BREEZE Open windows in the evening to circulate cool air in and warm air out. Try **running a large fan in the attic** during the evening when the windows are open to pull cool air through the house.

DRESS FOR THE WEATHER Wear loose, cool clothing so you don't need air-conditioning to counter the effects of too many layers. If necessary, ask your workplace to modify its dress code accordingly.

BE A/C SMART

If you do have air-conditioning, **work through this checklist** to make sure that your system is as energy-efficient as it can be:

- **make sure it's the right capacity** for your home—it's a waste of energy to have too powerful a system
- **seal its ducts** to maximize efficiency
- **clean or replace the filters** regularly
- **locate it well away from any heat-generating appliances**, which could make it work harder than necessary
- **keep windows and doors closed** when it's running, or the cooled air will escape
- **use it just to take the edge off the heat**, rather than creating a polar microclimate
- **turn it off about an hour before you go out**—the air will still be cool by the time you're ready to leave.

2 LIGHTING

A large proportion of the electricity we use is for lighting. Take advantage of natural sunlight and new technologies for brighter ways of lighting your home.

  **MAXIMIZE YOUR USE OF NATURAL LIGHT** For example, **paint walls in light colors** to brighten rooms, **keep draperies, shades, and blinds open** during the day to let in as much sunlight as possible, and **make sure your windows are clean**! If you work at home, **choose a naturally light room** to minimize the need for artificial task lighting.

  **LIGHT SWITCH** When you do need to use electric lighting, avoid old-fashioned incandescent bulbs, which are extremely inefficient. Halogen bulbs are better—about twice as efficient as incandescent ones—but for optimum efficiency **replace incandescent bulbs with low-energy compact fluorescent lightbulbs** (CFLs). Each CFL uses only about a quarter the electricity of an incandescent bulb, and they last up to ten times longer.

A GLIMPSE INTO THE FUTURE

Even more efficient, but less widely available, than CFLs are Light-Emitting Diodes (LEDs), which are small, solid, super-efficient lightbulbs. Because they don't have a filament, they're extremely durable: they last about ten times longer than CFLs and more than a hundred times longer than typical incandescent bulbs. Until recently, they were available only in specialist applications, such as electronic displays, but they're being used more and more for general lighting.

If you **fit a CFL** in a room where the light is on for an average of four hours a day, **it will pay for itself within a year**.

The world's largest lighting manufacturer, Philips, is planning to **phase out incandescent lightbulbs** in Europe and the U.S. **by 2016**.

Incandescent bulbs are an old technology—about **80% of the energy** used to create the light **escapes in the form of heat**.

A **worldwide switch to CFLs** would cause such a drop in electricity use that we could **close more than 250 coal-fired power plants**.

If you were to replace a quarter of your lightbulbs with CFLs you could **save around 50% on your lighting bill**.

If every household in the U.S. were to **switch one bulb to a CFL** they'd avoid the same amount of pollution as produced by **a million cars**.

In Australia the sale of **incandescent lightbulbs will be banned in 2010**. California is planning to phase them out by 2012.

If every British household installed **three CFLs**, they'd save enough energy to **power every streetlight** in the country.

IDENTIFY YOUR PRIORITIES It may not be feasible to replace all your incandescent bulbs at once, so prioritize the rooms that are lit for the longest periods. The energy required to produce an incandescent bulb is insignificant compared to the energy that it will waste over its lifetime, so it can make sense to replace incandescent bulbs even before they've burned out.

TURN LIGHTS OFF when you don't need them. If you're having a new house or extension built, **make sure that light switches are located near the door** to each room, to make it easier to switch off the lights when you leave the room.

USE A TASK LAMP to focus light just where you need it, rather than lighting up an entire room.

PLACE LAMPS IN THE CORNERS OF ROOMS, as they will reflect more light than if positioned more centrally along a wall.

PUT NIGHT LIGHTS ON A TIMER if you must have them on at night, and **make sure that your outdoor security lights have motion sensors** so that they come on only when they need to.

PIPE SUNLIGHT INTO YOUR HOME

You can take advantage of the sun's light by using sunpipes—tubes with super-reflective interior surfaces—to direct light from outside into dimly lit areas within a building. They were first used 4,000 years ago by the Egyptians, who used light shafts and mirrors to bring daylight down into the center of the pyramids. Modern equivalents are simple and relatively inexpensive: sunlight falling on a plastic dome on an exterior wall or roof is intensified down the tube and then diffused through an opaque light fixture. **Sunpipes can provide the equivalent of 100 watts of light in the winter and up to 500 watts on a sunny summer day**.

ELECTRONIC APPLIANCES

Modern homes are packed full of electronic devices—from games consoles to widescreen TVs. They may be using more power than you realize.

BE LABEL CONSCIOUS When you really do need to buy a new appliance, choose certified energy-efficient equipment. Look for the Energy Star logo in the United States, the Energy Saving Recommended logo in Britain, or the Eco-label (a flower with blue stars circling a green E) in the European Union.

LOOK FOR INTEGRATED APPLIANCES, such as integrated digital televisions (which combine a TV with a digital receiver). They have lower embodied energy (the energy embodied in their raw materials and manufacture) and use less energy to run than two separate appliances.

BUY AN INTELLIGENT CHARGER—look for ones labelled "-dV." These reduce their energy use to a trickle once the appliance is charged, rather than continuing to suck up energy.

TIME TO PRESS THE "STOP" BUTTON

We have more gadgets in our homes than ever before. They account for about **20% of the average American household electricity bill**), and that figure's expected to grow. Consumer electronics and information-communication technology are predicted to account for nearly half of all domestic energy usage by 2020, dwarfing everything except heating in their energy demand. All these clever gizmos add up to a huge carbon impact—not just from the electricity they run off, but also from their manufacture and disposal.

We urgently need to buck this trend by

- buying fewer appliances
- choosing more energy-efficient models
- using appliances more intelligently.

SWITCH OFF PROPERLY Televisions, videos, and other electronic equipment can use nearly as much energy when left on standby as when they're in use. To avoid wasting energy, unplug your equipment when you're not using it. Make things as easy as possible: **plug multiple devices into a power strip**, which will enable you to unplug them all at once.

USE CARBON-NEUTRAL GADGETS Look for solar-powered or clockwork products—for example, radios and chargers. As technologies develop, more and more of these appliances are coming onto the market each year.

REDUCE THE BRIGHTNESS of your TV screen. This can cut your TV's power consumption by 30–50%. The factory setting is often much brighter than necessary. If you have an LCD TV, you can usually **turn down the backlight**.

PICTURE PERFECT If you need to buy a new TV, consider energy efficiency. Rear-projection TVs tend to be the most efficient, followed by LCD models. Cathode-ray tube and plasma TVs are generally the least energy efficient.

KEEP TABS ON YOUR GADGETS

If you have trouble remembering to turn things off, a smart meter such as the PowerCost Monitor™ could help to remind you. Its digital display tells you exactly how many **kilowatt hours (kWh)** of electricity your home's using at any given time and how much is being added to your electricity bill as a result. Unlike conventional meters, it has a wireless display unit, which means that it's easy to monitor. Studies suggest that **smart meters can help households to cut their electricity use by up to 25%**—and they're a great way of keeping an eye on the kids' gadget use or quickly checking that you haven't left the iron or the broiler on before you leave the house!

Unplugging appliances could cut your electricity bills by up to 10%.

!

A study in California found that the average household has **19 appliances** on standby at any one time.

✓

Go small screen—a TV with a 20 in. screen can use up to 10 times less electricity than one with a 50 in. screen.

✓

In the U.S. 100,000 lb. of CDs become obsolete each month. **Download music** to avoid adding to this waste.

!

Electronic appliances left in **standby** mode account for **5%** of all domestic power consumption in the U.S., costing consumers $3.5 billion a year.

✓

Use a clockwork radio, rather than a 20-watt model, for 4 hours a day and save about 5½ lb. of CO_2 a year.

!

In the U.S. between 1950 and 2000, **electricity use per capita increased seven times over**.

CELLPHONES

Cellphones are becoming an ever more prominent part of modern life, and their contribution to energy demand is also growing at an alarming rate.

UNPLUG YOUR CHARGER when it's not in use. Even if nothing's attached, many chargers still use energy (if it feels warm, it's using electricity).

RESIST THE LURE OF REGULAR UPGRADES Cellphone companies are forever encouraging us to switch to the newest, most fashionable handset—usually long before the existing one's defunct. Avoid this waste of raw materials (and the energy that goes into manufacture) by choosing a robust model that will last.

PASS YOUR OLD PHONE ON to charity for recycling when you really do need a new one. Cellphones contain a cocktail of toxic substances. Recycling keeps these undesirable elements out of the waste stream and saves the mining and manufacturing impacts of making new handsets.

BE A CARBON HERO

You may soon be able to **use your cellphone to keep track of your travel-related carbon footprint**, thanks to an ingenious invention called the Carbon Hero™. Picking up a signal from your cellphone network, the keyring-size device is able to sense the length, speed, and mode of your journey. Using this information, it displays your associated personal carbon footprint (and the number of credits you'd need to buy to offset it; see p.9) on your cellphone. Since we tend to keep our cellphones with us at most times, the Carbon Hero™ can give a much more accurate "real time" reading of your carbon footprint than online carbon calculators, which tend to rely on you inputting general estimates about your daily activities.

Unless it's a -dv charger (see p.33), a phone **charger left plugged in** all the time will waste up to **95%** of the energy it consumes.

In Britain alone, **75,000** mobile phones are **dropped into the toilet** every year.

Unplug your phone charger when it's not in use and avoid emitting up to **15 lb.** of CO_2 each year.

In America each year one in three cellphone owners **replace their handset**.

The average cellphone contains around **30 elements**, including copper, lithium, lead, and chromium, which can be **toxic** in combination in landfill.

Cellphone chargers can use up to **5 watts** of electricity every hour when plugged in, even without the phone attached.

OVENS

Ovens can vary greatly in their energy consumption, so when it's time to get a new one, it's well worth seeking out the most efficient model available.

 **CHOOSE A GAS RANGE**, as these produce less than half the CO_2 emissions per kilowatt hour of electric ranges. **Look for one with electronic ignition**, which should use about 40% less gas than a model with a pilot light.

 **LOOK FOR A CONVECTION (OR FAN) OVEN**, which will enable you to cut cooking times by up to 30% and temperatures by around 20%.

 **USE THE MAIN OVEN ONLY WHEN NECESSARY** Cook small meals in a toaster oven broiler, which will use less than half as much energy.

 **GO MICRO** Microwave ovens can greatly reduce energy consumption for certain types of cooking, especially heating small portions and leftovers. However, they're a very inefficient way of thawing frozen foods (see p.44).

FUN IN THE SUN

For zero-emission cooking, try a **solar oven**, which allows you to bake, boil, or steam food in about the same time it would take on a normal stove, using only the sun's energy. They're ideal for picnics or camping trips—particularly in areas where fires are prohibited—or you could set one up in your yard throughout the summer. For cooking on cloudy days or at night, hybrid versions with an energy-efficient electric back-up are available.

Cooking accounts for just over **1%** of CO_2 emissions directly caused by our activities.

Cook meals from scratch: commercial food processing is responsible for about three times as much carbon emission as home cooking.

Self-cleaning ovens are more efficient than average, because they have extra insulation—but only if you don't use the self-cleaning function more than once a month.

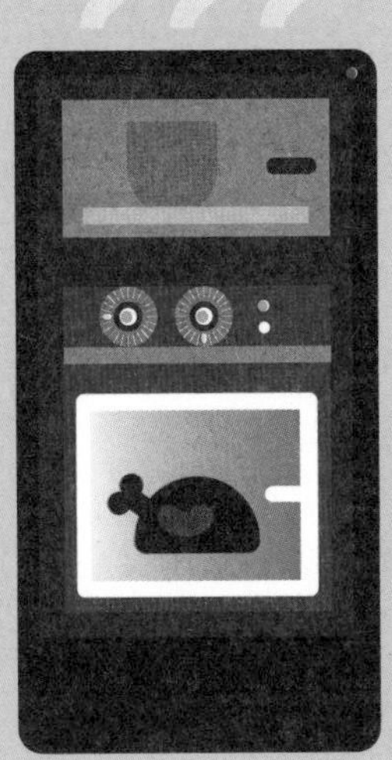

The average gas oven with a **pilot light uses as much gas** to keep the light constantly burning as to cook. Electronic ignition eliminates this waste.

10,000 people microwaving one meal each instead of using an electric oven would save enough energy to **heat a hot tub for a year**.

Turn your microwave off completely when not in use. If you don't, the digital clock could use almost as much energy over time as the microwave itself.

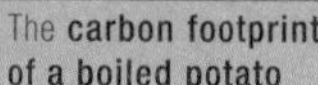

The **carbon footprint of a boiled potato** is more dependent on whether you cook it with the lid on or off than how and where it was farmed.

!

A gas range generates about **2 lb.** of greenhouse gas for every **10 quarts** of liquid boiled.

!

Placing a **6 in. pan** on an **8 in. burner** wastes **40%** of the burner's energy.

✓

Choosing the **right size pan** for cooking and **keeping the lid on** for most of the cooking process can reduce energy use by up to **90%**.

✓

Keep surfaces of cooking appliances **clean and shiny** to maximize the amount of heat that's reflected toward the food that you're cooking.

COOKING TECHNIQUES

Cooking food accounts for about 5% of the energy we use in our homes, so make sure your culinary skills aren't draining resources unnecessarily.

COOK IN BATCHES If you're cooking from scratch, prepare enough for several meals, and freeze or refrigerate the remaining portions. It will take much less energy (and time and effort) to reheat the leftovers than to cook new meals.

USE THE SMALLEST PAN POSSIBLE, because smaller pans require less energy.

MATCH THE PAN TO THE BURNER If the pan doesn't completely cover the burner, heat will be escaping around the sides.

USE FLAT-BOTTOMED PANS on electric elements to ensure maximum conduction.

WORK ON A NUMBER OF LEVELS Cook several items on top of each other in a stacked steamer to get the most out of each burner's energy.

IT AIN'T WHAT YOU DO ...

While getting the equipment right is important (see pp.38–9), it's actually the way that we cook food that has the bigger impact on energy use in the kitchen. A study by the United States Bureau of Standards has shown that some people use 50% less energy than others to cook the same meal.

A pop-up toaster uses up to **three times less energy** than the broiler in your oven.

  **NO MORE PREPACKAGED MEALS** When time's tight, and you're ready to reach for a prepackaged meal, why not cook a stir-fry instead? It will take a quarter of the time and energy—and that's not including the energy required to produce the prepackaged meal.

DON'T PREHEAT THE OVEN, unless you're making pastry, bread, or a soufflé. It should get hot quickly enough not to affect cooking times or quality.

LET IT BE Resist the temptation to open the oven door to check progress. Every time you do so, up to 25% of the heat escapes.

TURN OFF THE HEAT a few minutes before food's cooked—it'll continue cooking in the residual heat. Then, after you've taken your meal out, **supplement your heating system** by leaving the oven door open.

ALL UNDER ONE LID Cook whole meals in one pot. Delicious one-pot paellas, stews, dals, and casseroles use about a third of the energy of meals cooked in separate pans.

TIME IS ENERGY

Not surprisingly, anything we can do to reduce cooking times will generally save energy. In the hurly-burly of preparing the evening meal after work, try to bear in mind some of the following straightforward time- and energy-saving techniques:

- **keep pans covered** while cooking
- **chop food** into small pieces
- **defrost frozen food in the fridge** overnight rather than cooking from frozen
- unless you're using the cooking water to make soup, **use only enough water to cover the food** you're boiling
- **use a pressure cooker**: by building up steam pressure, these cookers cook at a higher temperature, reducing cooking time and using 50–75% less energy than a normal saucepan.

A notable exception to the "time is energy" principle is the energy-saving technique of **sit-boiling**, which can be used for cooking rice, pasta, and vegetables. As soon as the water is at a boil, put the food in the pan, cover with a tight-fitting lid, and turn the heat off completely. The food will cook in the residual heat, but will take around 50% longer than usual.

REFRIGERATION

Humming away 24/7, fridges and freezers account for about a quarter of domestic electricity consumption. So make sure they're not costing you or the environment more than necessary by using them as efficiently as possible.

LOCATION IS EVERYTHING Install your fridge or freezer in a cool spot, well away from your stove and any registers or radiators, with a gap of at least 2 in. for air to circulate behind it. Placing your appliance in a cool setting could cut associated CO_2 emissions by up to 350 lb. a year.

SPRING CLEAN Keep the coils at the back of your fridge or freezer dust-free. This will improve its efficiency by up to 30%.

CHECK YOUR TEMPERATURE Fridges don't need to be any cooler than 37–41°F and freezers do their job at 5°F. Any colder and they're wasting energy and your money. Invest in a fridge/freezer thermometer if there isn't one built in.

DEFROST REGULARLY (when the ice is ¼ in. thick). A frosted-up freezer uses more energy.

DOWNSIZE YOUR CHILLING

When it's time to replace your fridge, take a look inside your current appliance and ask yourself whether you need your next one to be as big.

- **Get a compact fridge** A small fridge, of 5 cubic feet or less, will hold more than you may think. Some of them have freezer compartments. Besides being cheaper to run, they are, of course, cheaper to buy.
- **Two for company** If you currently have a large refrigerator that you keep half-full most of the time, using its full capacity only when you are entertaining houseguests, consider replacing it with two compact fridges. Fill one of them with your everyday groceries and keep the other one unplugged except when you have guests and need the extra chilling space. **Just remember to empty and unplug it when they've left!**

CHECK THE DOOR SEAL by putting a piece of paper in the door. If it slips out when the door's closed, you may need to change the seal and/or door magnets, to stop cool air from escaping.

KEEP YOUR FRIDGE TIDY to help yourself find what you're looking for quickly. Up to 30% of the cool air held within the fridge escapes every time you open the door, so the quicker you can grab stuff and close the door, the better.

VACATION PREPARATION Before you go away, make sure your fridge is as empty as possible. If there are things that will last until you get back, turn the power down to chill these few items. Otherwise turn the fridge off completely.

TAKE IT OUT OF CIRCULATION Normally, passing on items you no longer want to people who can make use of them is a great way to save energy associated with the production of new goods. However, this principle doesn't apply to energy-guzzling old fridges and freezers. When you're replacing a decrepit fridge or freezer, don't put it on the secondhand market, but **send it to be dismantled by an approved recycler**.

FOOD FOR THOUGHT

You can take some of the burden off your fridge and freezer by being aware of the effects of the items you put in them. Here are some strategies to help you maximize efficiency:

- **Wait for food to cool before you put it in the fridge**, and make sure it's covered (ideally with a lid or plate rather than foil or plastic wrap). This not only stops your food from drying out, but stops the moisture it contains from condensing on the fridge/freezer walls, which makes the appliance use more energy and need defrosting more often.
- Plan ahead, so you don't need to use your oven or microwave to defrost frozen food. If you can **let frozen food thaw in the fridge overnight**, its chilliness will leave less work for the fridge to do.
- **Keep your fridge three-quarters full and freezer completely full** for optimum efficiency. This ensures that when you open the fridge there's less air to escape. Use newspaper to fill the freezer and keep water-filled plastic bottles in the fridge if you haven't got enough food to maintain the appropriate capacity.

Nearly **20%** of the energy generated worldwide is **used for refrigeration**.

The most efficient fridge-freezers are those with the **freezer above or below the fridge**. They use **10–25% less energy** than side-by-side models.

Unplugging an underused spare freezer can cut a home's CO_2 emissions by about **10%**.

Manual-defrost freezers use much less energy than auto-defrost models (so long as you defrost them regularly!).

Features such as **ice-makers and through-the-door water dispensers** can increase a fridge-freezer's energy use by up to **20%**.

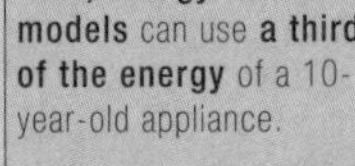

New, energy-efficient models can use **a third of the energy** of a 10-year-old appliance.

!

In the U.S. **30 million** plastic water bottles are **thrown away** each day.

✓

Support your local brewpub and you'll be rewarded with fresh, flavorful, packaging-free, zero-beer-mile beer.

!

A 33.8 oz. bottle of **Fiji Water** imported for sale in the U.S. requires 9 oz. of fossil fuel in its manufacture and transportation.

✓

Importing wine in bulk and bottling it at its destination, rather than at source, can reduce its carbon footprint by up to **40%**.

Leaving your **electric coffee maker** on "keep warm" all day could waste enough energy to make 12 cups of coffee.

!

Refillable plastic bottles are common in Scandinavia—you put your used bottles into a **reverse vending machine** and get back your deposit.

✓

Bottled water costs up to **10,000 times** as much as tap water.

!

Using a mug at work twice a day rather than disposable cups will avoid emitting around **100 lb.** of CO_2 a year.

✓

DRINKS

Whatever you're drinking, make sure it's not racking you up an excessive carbon footprint along with your bar bill.

BOIL ONLY AS MUCH WATER AS YOU NEED Completely filling the kettle just for one cup of tea releases an unnecessary 125 cups of CO_2. To take out the guesswork, **use a mug to pour in the required number of measures**.

BUY SHADE-GROWN COFFEE, which helps preserve ecosystems that sequester some of the CO_2 produced in making your daily brew.

DRINK A LOCALLY BREWED BEER and you'll enjoy a beverage of high quality and individuality and low "beer mileage."

TRY ORGANIC WINES, from as close to home as possible. You'll avoid the use of gallons of petroleum distillates and hundreds of pounds of petroleum-derived pesticides and cut the wine miles needed to shift this heavy treat.

CAP YOUR BOTTLED WATER CONSUMPTION

Chilled tap water tastes almost exactly the same as bottled mineral water, costs a tiny fraction of the price, and is delivered, packaging-free, by pipe, not truck. Keep a pitcher of it in the fridge. If you're worried about water quality, invest in a filtration system for your kitchen and have purified water literally on tap. To avoid having to buy bottled water when you're out, pack a small, robust drinking bottle and refill it en route.

Grow your own chamomile or mint for **herbal tea**, rather than always using factory-made tea bags.

4

DOING THE DISHES

Washing the dishes can be a tedious chore. Keep it quick, energy- and water-efficient, and carbon-light by getting into good habits at the sink or dishwasher.

  **HAND-WASH CAREFULLY** If done right, washing dishes by hand tends to be more energy-efficient than using a dishwasher—especially for small volumes of dishes. Instead of washing them under a running faucet, **put a plug in the sink**, or **use a plastic bowl**. And to minimize the amount of water you use when rinsing, **install a low-flow aerator** on your kitchen sink faucets.

 **SOAK FOOD-ENCRUSTED PANS** in soapy water before you wash them or put them in the dishwasher—that way, you'll use less water and energy overall to get them clean.

 **CHOOSE A WATER- AND ENERGY-EFFICIENT DISHWASHER** that's the right size for your lifestyle. **Look for one with a Soil Sensor**, which adjusts water and energy use depending on how dirty the dishes are in each load.

DISHWASHER WISDOM

Studies suggest that using a dishwasher can be more energy-efficient than washing dishes by hand. However, like many things in life, the energy- (and carbon-saving) benefits depend entirely on good technique. If you use a dishwasher:

- run it only when there's a **full load**—or, if you're desperate, use the half-load economy cycle
- use as **low** a **temperature** as possible
- **don't prerinse** items unless they're covered with burned- or dried-on food
- regularly **clean the filter** at the bottom of the machine
- **dry your dishes naturally** by opening the dishwasher before it begins the drying cycle; the hot dishes will dry quickly on their own
- **turn it off** when it's not in use—leaving the dishwasher on when it's not running can consume 70% as much power as it uses during the actual wash cycle.

A certified energy-saving dishwasher uses up to **40% less energy** than most older models, cutting carbon emissions by about **150 lb.** a year.

When washing dishes by hand, minimize the number of times you need to change the water by **washing the least-dirty items first**.

A **130°F** dishwasher cycle uses about **a third less energy** than a **150°F** cycle.

Running your dishwasher on an **economy setting** and halving the number of times you use it could cut your CO_2 emissions by over **200 lb.** a year.

!
Avoid aerosol sprays—they contain a high proportion of packaging to contents and are difficult to recycle.
✓
Dirt is good for you! Studies suggest that children who grow up in *too* clean an environment may be more susceptible to allergies and asthma.
✓
Tree-lined streets have up to two-thirds fewer dust particles in the air than streets without any form of vegetation.
✓
Use distilled white vinegar to clean faucets, windows, floors, tiles, etc., rather than buying specialized products.
✓
Buy cleaning products in bulk, and decant them into refillable smaller containers.

CLEANING PRODUCTS

The simple act of cleaning our homes has become an energy-intensive, product-laden process that can have an unnecessarily large environmental impact.

KEEP DIRT OUT Try planting trees or a hedge between your home and the street—the vegetation will capture a lot of dust before it reaches your home.

USE REUSABLE SPONGES AND CLOTHS or rags instead of paper towels or disposable wipes.

TRY MICROFIBER CLOTHS, which, when moistened, trap and absorb dust and dirt, avoiding the need for extra cleaning products.

CHOOSE PRODUCTS THAT WORK WELL AT LOW TEMPERATURES, such as floor cleaner that performs well with cold, rather than hot, water.

OPT FOR CONCENTRATED PRODUCTS to minimize the impacts of processing, transporting, and packaging your cleaning materials.

NATURE ABHORS A VACUUM!

The average vacuum cleaner uses ten times more electricity per hour than a computer—most of the energy is converted into heat, rather than suction. Be smart with your vacuum cleaner to minimize its carbon footprint:

- when choosing a new vacuum cleaner, **look for the most energy-efficient model** and make sure it takes reusable, rather than disposable, dust bags—even better, go for a bagless model
- **reduce the need to clean your floors** by placing doormats on each side of external doors, and take your shoes off when you come in
- **use a broom, dustpan and brush, or carpet sweeper** as a carbon-free alternative
- **compost the contents of your vacuum cleaner or dustpan** to avoid adding to landfill methane emissions.

PERSONAL HYGIENE & GROOMING

Whether your bathroom is a luxurious retreat or a morning battleground, it's likely that your household's bathing habits have a significant carbon footprint, which can be easily trimmed without leaving you grubby.

STICK TO SHOWERS The average bath contains about 20 gallons of water, whereas a five-minute shower uses about 8 gallons. **Save baths for special occasions**—pour yourself a glass of organic (and preferably local) wine, add a few drops of natural bath oil, light some soy candles (made without petrochemicals), and put on some soothing music.

KEEP YOUR SHOWERS SHORT If you spend much longer than five minutes in the shower you'll soon find you're using as much water as you would in the bath. **Use a shower timer** to remind you when your time's up.

GO WITH LOW FLOW Check your shower's flow by using it to fill a 2-quart pan. If it takes less than 12 seconds, install a low-flow shower head.

TOILET TACTICS

The process of collecting, purifying, and distributing tap water has a significant carbon footprint—about **4 oz. of CO_2 for every 100 gallons of water**. Yet we use it as though it were in limitless supply—often in the craziest ways. For example, up to a third of the drinking water that comes into the average Western home goes straight down the toilet, which is a ridiculous waste of this precious resource. To stem the flow, try putting some of these tips into action:

- **Put a plastic bottle filled with water into the cistern** to reduce the volume per flush (unless you already have a low-flow toilet). Or buy a toilet tank displacement device, which is designed for this purpose.
- If you're installing a new toilet, **specify one that uses low flush volumes** or allows you to choose flush volume according to "load."

The average person would save about 150,000 gallons of water over a lifetime by **turning it off while brushing their teeth**.

In the U.S., around **2 billion disposable razors are sent to landfill** every year.

A Japanese manufacturer has opened a factory in Mexico to supply **400,000 heated toilet seats a year** to the U.S. market.

Using a toilet tank displacement device will save about 1,300 gallons of water per year and will prevent the emission of about 3 lb. of CO_2.

Water heating accounts for around a quarter of the average home's energy usage.

Saving just 5 gallons of hot water per day will cut your energy usage by up to 700kWh per year, cutting CO_2 emissions by 300 lb.

INSTALL LOW-FLOW AERATING FITTINGS on your shower and faucets. These halve the flow and mix air bubbles into the water, which makes you feel that you're getting just as wet. A family of four can cut their CO_2 emissions by over 400 lb. a year by switching from a normal shower to a low-flow shower head.

TURN OFF THE FAUCET WHILE YOU BRUSH YOUR TEETH You'll save up to 2½ gallons of water each time you brush your teeth.

TAKE THE HEAT OFF YOUR HAIR Save yourself time in the morning, and cut your beauty regime's carbon footprint by having a low-maintenance haircut that doesn't need blitzing with a hair dryer or curling iron every day.

SHAVE AWAY YOUR CARBON FOOTPRINT Extend the life of your razor blades with a razor cartridge sharpener, which could cut down your razor consumption by up to 75%. Or move away from disposable blades: **buy a rechargeable electric shaver** or, best of all, **get to grips with a straight razor**. If looked after properly, it will give you a lifetime of smooth shaves.

- **Think about whether you really need to flush** every time you use the toilet.
- To avoid all the environmental (and financial) costs of using processed drinking water for flushing, **connect your toilet(s) to a rainwater harvesting unit or a system that recycles "gray" water** (water that's been used in sinks, bathtubs, showers, or the washing machine). Rainwater and "gray" water are of perfectly adequate quality for flushing the toilet.
- You could also **investigate toilets that separate the different kinds of waste going into them**, reducing the energy needed to convert "yellow," "gray," and "black" water into drinking-quality water.

LAUNDRY

Washing machines and tumble dryers certainly take the hard work out of doing the laundry, but they involve a lot of heating, so their carbon cost is high. Use them wisely, and your conscience will be as clean as your clothes.

INVEST IN AN ENERGY-SAVING MACHINE, which could cut your washing's energy consumption by up to a third. **Look for a machine with a high spin speed.** This will remove most of the water from your clothes, reducing the need for tumble drying (see p.56).

GO FROM TOP TO FRONT If your current washing machine is a toploader, buy a front-loading model when you need a replacement. Although toploaders tend to have a greater capacity, frontloaders use a fraction of the water and energy and treat clothes more gently.

PRESOAK ESPECIALLY GRUBBY CLOTHES before putting them in the washing machine to avoid the need for a hot wash and large amounts of detergent.

PRESSING MATTERS

Save time and energy by ironing only what you really need to. Ironing in large batches using a spray bottle filled with water, instead of the steam setting, will significantly cut your iron's energy use. And save the clothes that require a cooler iron until last. That way you can turn the iron off before you get to them and press them flat with the residual heat.

The average U.S. household washes around **6,000** items a year.

WASH FEWER LOADS Cutting down by just one wash per week can avoid around 50 lb. of CO_2 emissions each year. Wait until clothes actually are dirty before you wash them (hanging them up to air between wearings will help to keep them fresh) and then wait until you've got a full load to avoid wasting water and energy.

WASH AT LOWER TEMPERATURES Washing clothes at 30°C instead of a higher temperature uses up to 40% less energy, and your clothes will last longer. Seek out detergents designed to perform well at lower temperatures. This could cut your emissions by more than 400 lb. a year.

DRY WISELY When in operation, tumble dryers use more energy than almost any other household appliance, generating more than 6 lb. of greenhouse gas for each load they dry. So, while they're obviously convenient, they should be used only as a last resort. **Hang clothes up to dry** instead (outside, if possible—this makes them smell really fresh). If you must use a tumble dryer, **run loads back to back** while the drum's still warm, and **keep the lint collector and vent clear** for optimum efficiency.

WASHING ALL OVER THE WORLD

Up to 90% of the energy used for washing clothes goes into heating the water, so the temperature of your wash makes a huge difference to its carbon footprint.

Worldwide, people have very different washing habits. In Spain, 85% of laundry loads are washed at temperatures below 100°F, compared to just 4% in the UK, where the average wash temperature, 109°F, is around twice as hot as that in Japan and twice as many loads are put on each week than in Germany. And in the US, the average laundry temperature is just 84°F—55°F cooler than the European average.

!

The average U.S. washing machine is used **392 times** a year (or 7½ loads a week).

✓

Using a **washing line** instead of a tumble dryer could prevent 1,400 lb. of CO_2 emissions a year.

!

In the US, around **1,100 loads** of washing are started **every second**.

✓

An **Energy Star**-qualified washing machine uses up to **25 gallons less water** per load than a conventional model.

Washing machines and tumble dryers can account for up to **25%** of the electricity you use at home.

!

A **tumble dryer** with a blocked-up lint collector or vent can use up to 30% more energy than a well-maintained one.

!

Avoiding the **prewash setting** cuts each load's energy use by up to 15%.

✓

Calling all absent-minded ironers! If you need to buy a new iron, get one that **switches itself off** if left undisturbed for 10–15 minutes.

✓

Leaving a sprinkler on for an hour can consume the same amount of water as a family of four uses in a whole day.

Thanks to water-saving publicity campaigns, **water use in Finland has gone down by 40%** in the last 20 years.

An average American or Australian uses over **80 gallons** of water per day; a European around **40 gallons**; and a Gambian just over **1 gallon**.

The city of Cheyenne, Wyoming has established a **reclaimed water system** to irrigate its 230 acres of parks, cemeteries, and athletic fields.

5

WATER USE

We're using more water per person every year, and processing it requires huge amounts of energy, generating significant carbon emissions.

HARVEST THE RAIN Capture some of the rain that falls on your roof by connecting a water barrel to a downspout. This water can then be used in the garden. To take things further, **consider installing a rainwater harvesting system**, which collects and filters rain water for use in your toilet and washing machine.

USE WATER TWICE with a graywater system, which recycles water from bathtubs, showers, and washing machines. Or siphon bathwater into the garden for watering your plants.

WASH YOUR CAR WITH RAINWATER If you can't use rainwater, hand wash it, using a bucket of soapy water and a sponge or rag. If you really need to use a hose, **fit it with a nozzle**, so you can turn it off between rinses. This can save up to 200 gallons of water each time.

IRRIGATION INFORMATION

The type of plants that we put in our gardens and the way that we look after them can have a major bearing on the amount of water we use. Follow these water-saving irrigation tips, and your garden will thrive in all weathers:

- **plant drought-resistant species**—Mediterranean plants such as rosemary, lavender, and sage are very tolerant of long dry periods
- **water in the early morning or evening** to minimize evaporation
- **use a watering can**, rather than a sprinkler, and **aim water at the base** of your plants
- **keep grass long** (at least 1½ in.) to shade the soil and stop it from drying out
- **mulch around your plants** to help stop water from evaporating from the soil's surface, inhibit weed growth, and add nutrients.

BACKYARD

Spending time in a garden is the closest many of us regularly get to nature. And done the right way, gardening can actually reduce your carbon footprint.

 **RAKE UP DEAD LEAVES** instead of using a leaf blower—you'll save energy and tone your arms.

 **MOW THE GREEN WAY** Instead of using a gasoline-powered mower, go for an electric model (ideally using electricity from a renewable source; see p.13)—or, even better, a manual one.

 **PLANT TREES** if you have the space, or take part in your state's Arbor Day activities. A single tree can absorb more than a ton of CO_2 over its lifespan. When it dies and decays, much of this is released back into the atmosphere—so ideally, the tree should be used for lumber at the end of its life, and another planted in its place.

 **AVOID LIGHTING BONFIRES**, as they release CO_2 and other pollution. Compost your garden waste instead (see pp.62–3).

DON'T HEAT THE SKY

One of the world's most inefficient uses of energy, patio heaters have grown dramatically in popularity in recent years. To take the chill off entertaining outdoors, adopt this three-stage strategy:

- **keep blankets, shawls, and pullovers handy**
- **use a wood-fired brazier** if you're still cold
- and if it's *still* too chilly, **move indoors**!

A two-stroke lawn mower can produce as much pollution as **40 cars**.

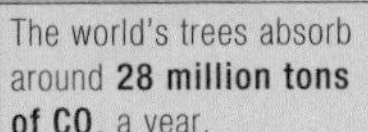

The world's trees absorb around **28 million tons of CO_2** a year.

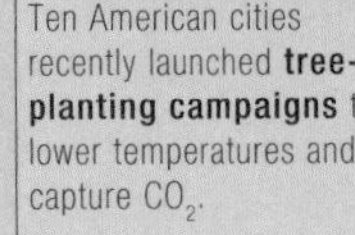

Ten American cities recently launched **tree-planting campaigns** to lower temperatures and capture CO_2.

!

In the U.S. each year, as much gasoline is spilled when **filling lawn mowers** as in the ***Exxon Valdez*** tanker disaster.

!

Used for just two hours, the average **patio heater** produces as much CO_2 as a car does in an average day.

Plant some bamboo, as it stores more CO_2 and generates 35% more oxygen than an equivalent area of trees.

!

The average American generates about **4 lb. of garbage** each day.

✓

In Dhaka, Bangladesh, **all organic waste is composted**, reducing methane emissions by **1,400 tons** a year, generating jobs and cleaning up the city.

!

A **quarter of methane emissions** are due to organic waste rotting in landfills.

✓

Composting organic waste from the home saves approximately **30%** of our trash from going to the landfill.

In 1998, the U.S. generated **22 million tons** of food residuals and **composted only 2%** of that waste.

!

Composting worms eat at least **half their body weight** in organic matter every day.

✓

Around **60%** of the average household's refuse consists of **biodegradable** food, garden, and paper waste.

!

Composting your organic waste could cut CO_2 emissions by up to **700 lb.** a year, equivalent to around **750–1,000 miles of car travel**.

✓

COMPOST

In a landfill, organic waste decomposes without oxygen, which causes it to give off methane, a potent greenhouse gas with 21 times the impact of CO_2. Composting averts this problem and creates natural fertilizer and soil conditioner.

  **MAKE YOUR OWN COMPOST** Buy a simple composting bin, or make your own: a wooden frame covered with old carpet or plastic sheeting to retain moisture and heat.

 **EQUIP YOUR KITCHEN WITH A BOKASHI BUCKET** This ingenious Japanese composter will deal with almost any kind of waste food (including cooked food, meat, fish, and dairy products) and is small enough to fit in the kitchen. It takes only a few weeks to break down your organic waste into soil improver for your garden and liquid fertilizer for your houseplants.

 **SET UP A WORM FARM**, a self-contained composting unit containing tiger worms, which convert organic matter into vermicompost—a superb natural soil conditioner and plant food.

HEAPS OF ADVICE

For the best composting results, follow these simple guidelines:

- **add roughly equal amounts of nitrogen-rich "green" matter**, such as plants, leaves, grass clippings, and vegetables, **and carbon-rich "brown" matter**, such as cardboard, paper, and twigs
- besides the materials listed above, **you can also compost** sawdust, bread, eggshells, tea bags, coffee grounds and filter papers, hair and lint, farm manure, and vacuum cleaner bags
- **but don't compost** big branches, painted wood, sawdust from plywood, colored or coated paper, meat, fish, dairy products, diseased plants, or waste and litter from carnivorous pets
- **turn the compost every few weeks** to make sure it rots down properly without producing methane.

5 GROWING YOUR OWN

Besides buying local, seasonal, organically produced food, try growing your own. You'll cut back even more on food miles and packaging, save money, savor the flavor, and reconnect with the earth.

GROW ORGANICALLY, avoiding petrochemical-based fertilizers and pesticides—and the greenhouse gases released in their production.

START A MICRO-GARDEN For example, grow herbs on your kitchen windowsill, salad leaves in window boxes, or tomatoes in pots.

PLANT SOME FRUIT TREES You'll reap an abundance of free, organic fruit, and the trees will absorb CO_2 as they grow.

GROW YOUR OWN FLOWERS Avoid the CO_2 emissions associated with flowers grown in hothouses and flown vast distances. Plant bulbs, take cuttings of long-lasting shrubs, or plant patches of native wildflowers, which need minimal watering or other attention.

IF YOU HAVEN'T GOT A GARDEN ...

See if there is a **community garden** in your area. There are currently around 10,000 of them in American cities, including one in the heart of Midtown Manhattan. With a few hours' attention each week, a little patch of land could change the way your whole family eats.

If there aren't any gardens (or plots)—or if you'd prefer not to be in sole charge of your crops—look for a **Community Supported Agriculture (CSA)** program in your area. These enable you to become involved in a local farm in return for a share of the harvest. Your involvement can take the form of a financial investment or time spent working on the farm—or you can simply buy your food directly from the farm (see p.72).

✓

Home-grown produce can be eaten minutes after being picked—when it's at its **most nutritious**.

✓

A single **apple tree** can produce up to 500 apples per season for 20 years.

✓

During World War II, **"victory gardens"** planted across the U.S. supplied up to 40% of all vegetables consumed by American civilians.

!

Tending lawns in the U.S. uses around 320 billion gallons of water a week—enough to water **12 million acres of organic vegetables** all summer.

In 2006, **79%** of fresh flowers sold in the U.S. were imported.

Take cuttings, rather than buying new plants, to cut back on transportation, avoid building up a mountain of plastic pots, and save money.

Make mini-greenhouses, or cloches, for your seedlings by cutting the base off plastic bottles.

Community Supported Agriculture farms are running throughout the world, with up to 3,000 in North America alone.

!

Producing 1 ton of **cement** releases around 1,500 lb. of CO_2 into the atmosphere. Cement production accounts for about 5% of man-made CO_2 emissions.

✓

Converting a million rooftops into **green roofs** could prevent the emission of around 600,000 tons of CO_2.

On average, using a cubic yard of **wood** generates 1 ton less CO_2 than using the same volume of other building materials.

✓

Make an art of **salvaging**—a great way to save money, keep valuable materials out of landfill, and give your building project a **unique character**.

✓

A school in Sheffield, England, has been **super-insulated**—far beyond any official regulations—with 4,000 pairs of **recycled jeans**.

✓

A ton of **recycled steel** requires 1,500 lb. less iron ore, 1,000 lb. less coal, 75% less energy, and 40% less water than a ton produced from scratch.

✓

BUILDING MATERIALS

Whether you're doing a simple home improvement or commissioning a dream home, try to minimize the energy that goes into making your building (its "embodied energy") and use building materials with a low carbon footprint.

WOOD FOR GOOD Use wood instead of other building materials wherever you can. Not only do trees absorb CO_2, but in its processing wood has the lowest energy consumption and the lowest CO_2 emissions of any common building material. It's also a great insulator. Make sure to **use reclaimed or sustainably produced lumber**.

AVOID CEMENT—one of the most energy-intensive products in the world. If you need to use cement or concrete, try to source a material made from a cement substitute, such as fly ash or slag.

STRAW HOUSE Use carbon-neutral and super-insulating straw bales stacked within wooden frames to create buildings that are up to three times as energy-efficient as traditional models.

GREEN YOUR ROOF

More and more people are creating "green roofs" by planting their roofs with vegetation. Green roofs provide excellent insulation. The plants absorb solar radiation, which stops it from entering the building—this is particularly desirable in cities, where the "heat island" effect can raise local temperature by up to 10%. They also reduce storm-water runoff and provide habitats for a broad range of plants and creatures.

Buy work surfaces, table tops, or doors made out of **recycled plastic**.

EATING LOCAL

The food you've eaten today may well have traveled thousands of miles to your plate, clocking up significant carbon emissions en route. Reduce your gastro-impact by choosing locally produced, seasonal food whenever you can.

GROW YOUR OWN FOOD and trim food miles down to food feet (see pp.64–5).

STREET PLAN When it's time to plant seeds, coordinate with like-minded neighbors so that you don't all grow the same crops. This way, you'll be able to share a range of produce, rather than having a glut of one or two crops.

BECOME A "LOCAVORE" There is a growing movement of people, known as "locavores," who restrict their diet to foods sourced within a certain range—for example, a radius of 100 miles. Why not try joining them? If you find this ruling too strict, don't be afraid to allow yourself occasional treats, such as tropical fruit, from farther afield, and apply this rule primarily to everyday foodstuffs.

REAL GOOD FOOD

We've gotten used to eating what we want whenever we want it, ignoring the fact that transporting out-of-season food thousands of miles has a huge environmental impact. The benefits of buying local, seasonal food are varied and considerable:

- it **cuts back on the environmental impacts** of transportation
- it generally **requires less energy-hungry packaging, processing, and refrigeration**
- it's **fresher, tastier, and more nutritious** (long-distance produce is often picked before it has ripened to help it survive the lengthy journey)
- **more varieties are available**—not just the ones that can withstand long trips
- it **supports small local growers** and brings money into your local economy.

SHOP LOCALLY Make sure you're not adding to your groceries' carbon footprint by making unnecessary car journeys to out-of-town shopping centers: minimize car trips, and shop close to home.

BUY IN SEASON and enjoy a constantly changing parade of produce that's locally produced and at its prime throughout the year. Eating local and seasonal could cut your carbon footprint by as much as 1,500 lb. a year.

CELEBRATE SEASONAL FOOD by attending local food fairs and festivals.

HAVE A JAM SESSION To enjoy your favorite foods all year round without flying them in from the other side of the world when they're out of season, buy them in bulk when they are in season, and make delicious relishes, jellies, and jams with them.

SPREAD THE WORD Invite your friends to a locally sourced dinner to show them how well you can eat using just local, seasonal ingredients.

GREENHOUSE EFFECT

Locally grown produce doesn't always have a lower carbon footprint than the same food grown thousands of miles away. The pressure to supply fruit and vegetables out of their normal season is persuading some farmers in cold-climate countries to grow crops such as tomatoes in heated greenhouses in early spring or late fall. This can use as much, if not more, energy than transporting them from sunnier climes. Resist both of these heavy carbon consumers, and enjoy seasonal produce when nature intended you to—good food comes to those who wait.

In North America, ingredients travel an average of **1,500 miles** from farm to plate.

!

It takes **5 lb. of wild fish** to produce **1 lb. of farmed fish**. Global fishing fleets are directly responsible for over **140 million tons of CO_2** emissions a year.

✓

The average American could do more to reduce global-warming emissions by becoming a **vegetarian** than by switching to a hybrid car (see p.120).

!

Producing **1 lb. of meat** is responsible for more greenhouse emissions than going for an **hour's drive while leaving all the lights on** at home.

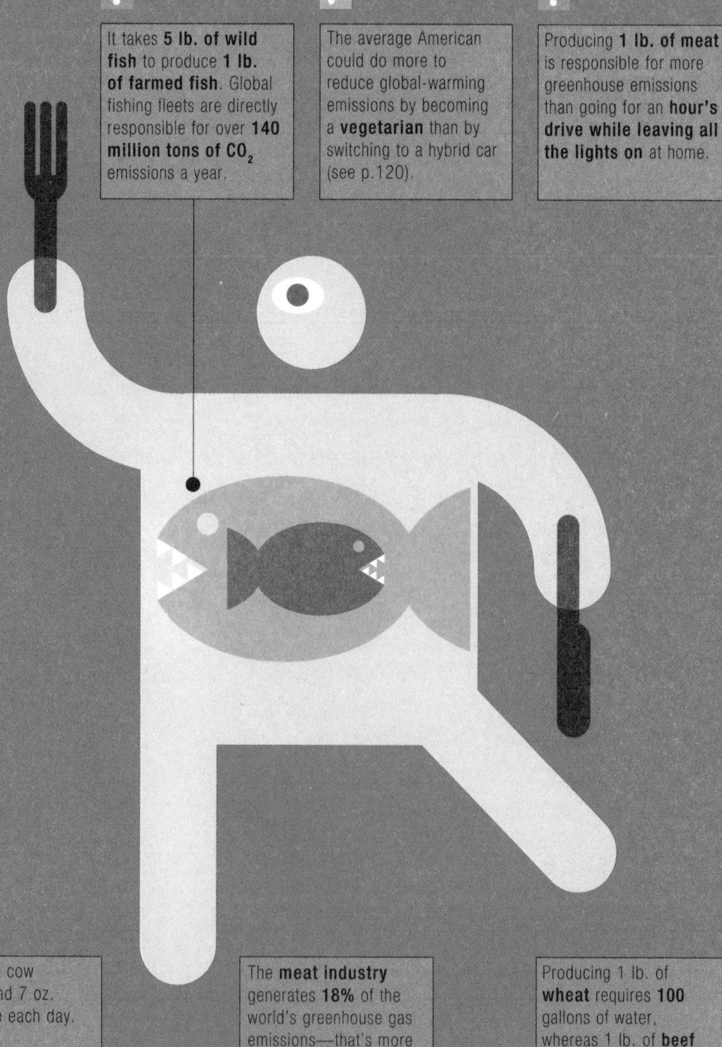

The average cow expels around 7 oz. of **methane** each day.

!

The **meat industry** generates **18%** of the world's greenhouse gas emissions—that's more than from all forms of transportation.

!

Producing 1 lb. of **wheat** requires **100** gallons of water, whereas 1 lb. of **beef** requires up to **25,000** gallons.

!

FOOD CHAIN

The carbon footprint of food is affected not only by the distance it has traveled but also by the amount of energy required to produce it. Animal products, particularly meat, are among the most resource-hungry items on the menu.

GO VEGGIE By avoiding meat altogether, you can cut the CO_2 associated with your diet by about half. For maximum impact, **cut down on dairy products**, too. If cutting out meat completely sounds too drastic, try eating a bit less. For every pound of beef you avoid you'll trim your carbon footprint by up to 13 lb. of CO_2.

QUALITY, NOT QUANTITY If you cut down the amount of meat you eat, you'll be able to afford higher quality, organic, locally produced meat. It will have a lower carbon footprint, and should taste much better!

LAY OFF FISH Apart from depleting fish stocks by overfishing, the fishing industry uses huge amounts of fuel for its trawlers. Help to reduce demand by reducing your consumption.

WHAT'S THE BEEF?

In the last 50 years, **global meat production has increased fivefold**, and the amount of meat eaten per person has doubled. This has put a heavy burden on the environment, as it requires much more land and water, as well as about ten times more energy, to produce animal than vegetable protein. One of the biggest impacts of meat production is the large amount of methane expelled by livestock. **Methane is around 21 times more potent as a greenhouse gas than carbon dioxide**, and 37% of human-created methane emissions come from the livestock sector. Add to this the collateral damage associated with deforestation for pasture, production of fertilizers for feed crops, and energy to run meatpacking plants, and your doctor's advice to eat less meat obviously makes sense for the environment, as well as for your arteries!

DIRECT BUYING

Running to the supermarket is a convenient way to stock your kitchen cabinets, but the carbon impacts are high. Buying direct from producers can trim your groceries' carbon footprint and also save you money.

SHOP AT A LOCAL FARMERS' MARKET that restricts the provenance of produce on sale to a radius of 100 or even 50 miles (in contrast to the 1,000-mile-plus journey of many supermarket items). Or **seek out local farm stands** to buy direct from the producer.

JOIN A CSA BOX PROGRAM—a weekly delivery of organic, seasonal food within a limited radius. **Look for a CSA (Community Supported Agriculture) farm** in your area (see p.64).

BEAUTY COMES FROM WITHIN By insisting on "perfect" produce, supermarkets force farmers to waste huge amounts of delicious food—and the energy required to grow it. Let local traders know you're happy to buy strange-looking fruit and vegetables.

SKIP THE SUPERMARKET

Supermarket shopping can come at a high price to the environment:

- In order to provide large volumes of standard products, supermarkets tend to buy produce at rock-bottom prices, often from **overseas suppliers**.
- Even a product grown relatively locally may have traveled hundreds—or even thousands—of miles from farm to shop via a number of different locations for **processing, packaging, storage, and distribution**.
- Strict requirements for uniform appearance mean that **large proportions of each crop are often rejected**.

You can avoid the excessive costs (to you and the environment) of buying from supermarkets and their middlemen by **buying food directly from the grower**.

Around **900 million tons** of food are shipped around the planet each year, four times the amount that was shipped in 1961.

Between 1994 and 2006, the value of U.S. agricultural products **directly sold** increased 37% from $592 million to $812 million.

Food production, processing, distribution, and preparation consumes up to **20%** of the U.S. energy supply.

It's estimated that for every ton of bananas shipped, **two tons of waste** is left behind on the plantations.

Produce from farm shops, farmers' markets, and CSA box programs can be up to **40% cheaper** than food bought from supermarkets.

✓

The world organic market has been growing by **20% a year** since the early 1990s. Organic food sales totaled **$23 billion** in 2002.

✓

Organic **potatoes** have statistically significantly higher levels of vitamin C, magnesium, iron, and phosphorous than nonorganic equivalents.

World consumption of chemical **pesticides and fertilizers** has risen from 30 million tons a year in 1960 to 150 million in 2000.

!

Approximately **75 million acres** of land worldwide are now farmed organically.

✓

Organic produce contains less water than conventional equivalents, so you're getting more food for your money than you may think.

✓

Organic farms have been found to contain 85% more **plant species**, 33% more **bats**, 17% more **spiders**, and 5% more **birds** than nonorganic ones.

✓

ORGANIC PRODUCTS

Organic farming is experiencing a surge in popularity as consumers recognize the benefits of food produced without energy-intensive synthetic fertilizers and pesticides, plant-growth regulators, and livestock-feed additives.

DRINK ORGANIC MILK If you can't switch all your food to organic, milk is a good place to start. The price difference is marginal, but organic milk uses only a third of the energy needed to produce the nonorganic version. It also contains higher levels of nutrients (for example, 60–70% more omega 3 essential fatty acids) than intensively-farmed milk.

GET THE BALANCE RIGHT Organic isn't *always* the best choice: highly packaged, air-freighted organic produce will ratchet up a hefty carbon footprint en route. Try to find food that's seasonal, local, unpackaged, and unprocessed. And if it's also organic, that's even better!

LOOK FOR NON-FOOD ORGANIC PRODUCTS, including textiles (see pp.76–7) and toiletries.

GREAT TASTE, LOW CO_2

Conventional farming uses huge amounts of fossil-fuel based fertilizer, which leads to the emission of significant levels of greenhouse gases in both its manufacture and application. In contrast, **organic soils capture and store up to 30% more CO_2 than soils from conventional farms**. If all the corn and soybeans grown in the U.S. were farmed organically, 500 billion lb. of CO_2 would be removed from the atmosphere each year.

One average-sized organic farm can absorb **120 cars' worth** of CO_2.

CLOTHING

Striding out in this season's designs may turn heads, but the behind-the-scenes impact could be messy. Choose carefully and look after your clothes to minimize the carbon emissions of looking good.

 **BUY TO LAST** Choose well-made garments you really like and will wear for years—**avoid fast fashion**. To avoid the energy costs and resource use of producing new items, **opt for vintage clothing**—it's cheaper and usually better made than quick-turnover fashion.

 **SWAP** Instead of splurging on new outfits, host a clothes-swapping party with your friends.

  **LOOK AFTER YOUR WARDROBE** Have clothes repaired—or even restyled (designers are becoming increasingly adept at fashioning new items out of the best parts of worn garments).

 **RECYCLE CLOTHES** that are beyond restyling or repair. They can be shredded and rewoven into new items through a textile-recycling program.

LOW-CO_2 TEXTILES

Look for items made from the following types of eco-friendly fiber:

- **recycled materials**—fleece jackets can be made from plastic bottles, and running shoes from denim and car tires
- **organic cotton and wool**
- **bamboo or hemp fiber**—these are both naturally fast-growing plants that absorb above-average levels of CO_2 and require minimal application of fertilizer and pesticides.

In contrast, **avoid synthetic fabrics** such as nylon and polyester, which are made from petrochemicals in very energy-intensive processes. Nylon manufacture produces nitrous oxide, a greenhouse gas 310 times more potent than CO_2.

✓

An acre of **bamboo** can absorb more than 1,500 lb. of CO_2 each year.

✓

It takes just **25 half-gallon plastic bottles** to make one adult-size **fleece jacket**.

It takes **ten times** more energy to make a ton of textiles than a ton of glass.

!

Wash clothes at a low temperature, and avoid tumble drying (see pp.55–7). This will help your clothes to last longer (and save electricity, of course).

✓

Up to 15% of Americans shop at **consignment or resale stores**, preventing 2½ billion lb. of textiles from entering the waste stream each year.

✓

Cotton is the world's most polluting crop, accounting for up to a quarter of all agrichemical use, including 50,000 tons of pesticides each year.

!

6 BUYING LESS

Everything you buy in the stores, from radishes to hairclips, has taken energy to grow or extract, manufacture, package, transport, and sell. So, by finding ways to curb your consumption, you can cut your carbon footprint.

 **EAT BEFORE YOU SHOP FOR FOOD** Studies show that this helps trim the amount you buy.

 **THINK LONG TERM** Investing in high-quality durable goods is cheaper in the long run, and less wasteful than buying cheap, throwaway versions.

 **BUY SERVICES INSTEAD OF PRODUCTS**—such as leasing services for office equipment, so manufacturers will produce durable, updatable products, rather than ones that are obsolete in a few years.

 **AVOID DISPOSABLES**, which invariably have a high carbon impact. For example: **cover food with a dish, plate or lid** instead of foil or plastic wrap; **use hand towels and dish**

RETAIL DETAILS

The average Western shopaholic adds more than **3 tons of CO_2** to their carbon footprint each year simply by buying stuff. Without full "life cycle assessment," which looks at the impacts of every stage of a product's life, it can be very difficult to work out the relative carbon footprints of different items. But generally, when it comes to reducing the consumption component of your carbon footprint, less is definitely more. Besides avoiding overpackaged items and buying locally produced (ideally organic) produce, buying fewer, more durable things, reusing and repairing them, and choosing second-hand where possible can cut the impacts of your buying habits dramatically.

In nature there's no such thing as waste—every natural material, once it's fulfilled one function, is useful in another way. With easy access to plentiful

towels instead of paper towels; and **buy sturdy, reusable utensils and dishes** for barbecues and picnics, instead of flimsy disposables.

DO SOME REAL FEEL-GOOD SHOPPING Massages, beauty treatments, and concert tickets are great junk-free treats.

FIX THINGS, instead of throwing them away at the first sign of wear or malfunction. **Look for specialist repair shops** in your area, or learn a new skill yourself, such as furniture upholstery or renovation.

FIND A NEW LEASE ON LIFE Try selling unwanted items online (for example, on eBay), donating them to a new home (try Freecycle or Craigslist) or swapping them with neighbors via a community swap shop. These forums could also help you find things you need.

MAKE SURE NEW THINGS WILL LAST Check that items of hardware can be easily repaired and that the manufacturer will supply spare parts. It may be worth investing a little more in products with long guarantees.

goods, we tend to forget this basic principle, and **we throw away 80% of all manufactured products we buy within six months of purchase**. Besides reducing the amount you buy, think laterally, and try to find as many uses as possible for everything you've bought before you throw it away.

On average, U.S. households **waste 14%** of their food purchases.

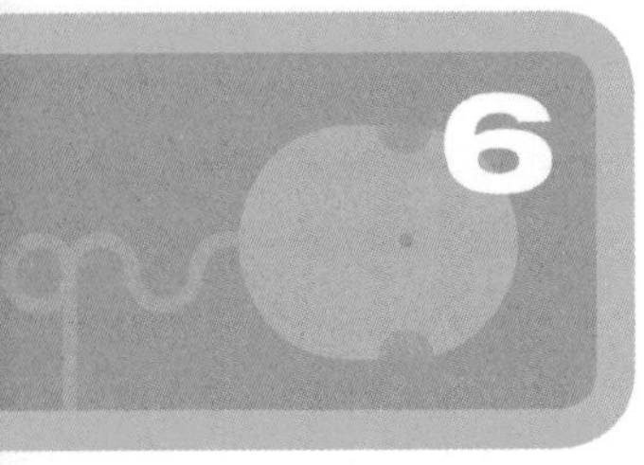

6 INTERNET SHOPPING & SERVICES

Take advantage of the hugely expanding range of services available online to cut emissions and other waste, and save yourself time and money. Just remember to turn the computer off when you've finished!

MANAGE YOUR FINANCES ONLINE Online bill paying and banking help avoid unnecessary energy use from paper production, printing, postage, and waste disposal. And generate a lot less paperwork to clutter up your home …

PROCEED TO CHECKOUT If you really need to use a supermarket and would normally drive to it, try buying from its website instead. This is much less fuel-intensive (especially if there's a facility for you to specify a delivery time when other deliveries are being made in your area) and saves a great deal of time and stress.

DOWNLOAD MUSIC from the Internet and put it on an mp3 player. Once you've worked out how to track down your favorite tunes online, you need never buy another CD.

GREENER ONLINE SHOPPING

If you can't get the products you need locally, buying goods online can be an environmentally friendly and timesaving way to shop. When buying from the cyber aisles, minimize your environmental impact in the following ways:

- **avoid requesting next-day delivery**, as this requires energy-guzzling individual delivery trips
- **combine orders with friends, relatives, and colleagues** to save on postage and unnecessary journeys
- **have orders delivered to your workplace**, where they can always be accepted—this avoids items having to be re-sent if you're not at home when they arrive.

!

In the U.S. **540 million printed Yellow Pages directories** are distributed each year.

✓

Ask not to receive a phone book and **look up numbers online** instead. You'll save paper and be guaranteed up-to-date information.

✓

Around **35 million** U.S. consumers pay their bills online.

✓

If all Americans received and paid their bills online, they'd save **18.5 million trees'-worth of paper** each year.

!

Change your online passwords regularly, and trash unsolicited e-mails purporting to be from your bank that ask you to divulge sensitive information.

✓

American companies could save **$200 million** collectively each day if they switched to **paperless billing**.

✓

One delivery round by a supermarket **delivery van** can remove the need for 20 separate car journeys to the supermarket.

!

Every year, Americans use enough **plastic wrap** to cover Texas.

!

In the U.S., we use more than **80 billion aluminum drinks cans** every year.

An average American family of four uses almost **1,500 plastic bags** a year.

!

The average person could cut their carbon emissions by **1,200 lb.** a year by reducing their packaging waste by 10%.

✓

Americans throw away **25 billion** polystyrene cups each year.

!

A robust, reusable bag needs to be used only **11 times** to have a lower environmental impact than using 11 disposable plastic bags.

✓

CUTTING THE WRAP

It's likely that a significant proportion of the contents of your garbage can consists of food packaging. Before you even think about recycling (see pp.85–7), make sure you're avoiding as much waste as possible every time you shop.

BUY NONPERISHABLE ITEMS IN BULK One large package requires less energy to make than a lot of small ones. Even better, **buy them loose**, and put them in your own reusable containers.

CHOOSE PRODUCTS SOLD IN REFILLABLE CONTAINERS, and make the effort to reuse them. Ask your favorite brands and stores to stock this kind of packaging if they don't already.

GIVE IT BACK Make your feelings known by unwrapping overpackaged purchases in the shop, and ask the staff to deal with the waste.

GO EASY ON THE FOIL Aluminum production is resource- and energy-intensive. So use foil sparingly, reusing it where possible. Then recycle it to recoup the valuable resources it contains.

MAKE DISPOSABLE BAGS HISTORY

Worldwide we carry home between 500 billion and a trillion plastic bags every year. **That's up to 150 bags a year for every person on Earth, or 2 million a MINUTE.**

It takes 11 barrels of crude oil to produce a ton of plastic bags, but paper bags aren't much better—it takes 17 trees to produce a ton of them.

A **tax on plastic shopping bags** in the Republic of Ireland has cut their use by more than 90%.

AVOID PACKAGING MADE FROM MIXED MATERIALS, such as plastic and foil—it's harder to recycle.

REUSE PLASTIC CONTAINERS from take-out meals or from store-bought foods.

AVOID SINGLE SERVINGS The packaging and processing that goes into them gives them a huge environmental footprint—an individual serving of coffee has ten times as much packaging as the equivalent coffee sold in bulk.

PACK YOUR OWN LUNCH in reusable containers. You'll save money and avoid generating 7 oz. or more of empty single-serve yogurt tubs, juice cartons, and sandwich bags each day.

AVOID POLYSTYRENE—it's made from valuable petrochemicals and doesn't biodegrade; and because it's so bulky, transportation and processing are expensive, so widespread recycling is unlikely to be feasible.

THANK COMPANIES that have switched to more compact, biodegradable, or recycled packaging.

Although plastic bags may make a relatively minor contribution to your carbon footprint, it's incredibly easy to prevent the wasted resources and landfill problems that they cause by packing carefully, and **bringing your own reusable hemp, organic cotton, or canvas bags with you every time you shop**. Using your own bag instead of just a modest four disposable plastic bags per week will cut your annual carbon footprint by about 18 lb.

Biodegradable plastic bags made from maize or tapioca starch are a better option than normal plastic bags. They quickly break down into harmless elements, instead of lingering for hundreds of years like their petrochemical counterparts. However, their manufacture still uses large amounts of energy and other resources, so **you're really much better off with a reusable bag** whenever possible.

RECYCLING

Everything you throw away has a carbon footprint—created through its production and, ultimately, its disposal. So try to reduce the amount you chuck—by buying less and reusing things, then recycling as much as you can of what's left.

KEEP A LOW PROFILE The average adult receives 42 lb. of unsolicited mail a year. Register with a mail preference service and **always check the "don't pass on my address" box** when filling out applications.

SHARE NEWSPAPERS AND MAGAZINES with colleagues or neighbors, rather than always buying your own, and **try to find a second use for them**—for example, as wrapping paper—before you recycle them.

TURN OVER AN OLD LEAF Every ton of paper reused or recycled prevents the emission of over a ton of CO_2, keeps 100 $ft.^3$ of waste out of landfill, saves enough energy to light the average home for six months, and leaves 17 trees standing, busy absorbing CO_2.

THE BENEFITS OF RECYCLING

Waste prevention and recycling help reduce greenhouse gas emissions in a host of ways—some less obvious than others:

- It **diverts organic waste from landfills**, avoiding the production of methane (a greenhouse gas 21 times more potent than CO_2), which is released when organic matter decomposes anaerobically (without oxygen).
- It **cuts down on incineration**, reducing greenhouse gas emissions from the combustion of waste.
- It **saves energy**—reusing products or making them with recycled, rather than virgin, materials requires less energy for extraction, transportation, processing, and manufacturing, so less CO_2 is emitted. For example, recycled glass uses up to 50% less energy, recycled

BE VIRTUOUS WITH YOUR VITREOUS Recycling just one glass bottle saves enough energy to power a television for 90 minutes.

RECYCLE PLASTIC BOTTLES Plastic is difficult to recycle, since it comes in so many different forms, or polymers. But with 8% of world oil production going into plastics, we need to recoup what we can. PET plastic bottles (identified by a number 1 inside a triangle) are a good place to start—recycling just one saves enough energy to power a 14-watt compact fluorescent lightbulb for over 25 hours.

YES CAN DO Producing an aluminum can from recycled material takes only 5% of the energy needed to make it from virgin raw materials—recycling just one can saves enough energy to run a computer for three hours.

BUY RECYCLED PRODUCTS, such as recycled paper or toilet paper, or fleeces made from recycled plastic bottles.

SPEAK OUT Ask suppliers to design packaging that can be reused and/or recycled.

paper products around 60–70% less energy, and recycled aluminum a whopping 95% less energy, than their equivalents made from virgin materials.

- It **increases storage of carbon in trees**—plants absorb CO_2 from the atmosphere and store it, a process called **carbon sequestration**. Waste prevention and recycling of paper products allow more trees to remain standing in the forest, where they can continue removing CO_2 from the atmosphere.

Up to 80% of the contents of the average household trashcan are recyclable. For every pound of waste you recycle, you can reduce CO_2 emissions by at least a pound. If you're currently pretty wasteful, cutting back and recycling could cut your annual carbon footprint by up to a ton.

!

In the U.S., the amount of aluminum thrown away could rebuild the country's **entire commercial air fleet** every three months.

!

The average trashcan contains enough unrealized energy for **500 baths** each year.

✓

Some countries, such as Belgium, Switzerland, and Finland, have a **glass recycling rate of over 90%**—more than four times higher than in the U.S.

States with bottle deposit laws have **35–40% less litter** by volume.

✓

The **global aluminum industry** uses as much electric power as the continent of Africa.

!

Recycling just two glass bottles saves enough energy to boil water to make **five cups of coffee**.

✓

Americans throw away the equivalent of more than **30 million trees in newsprint** every year.

!

7 BABY CARE

Looking after a baby is one of the most fulfilling—and exhausting—things most of us will ever do. As you celebrate your child's milestones, keep one eye on the carbon impact of caring for him or her, and do what you can to minimize it.

  **BREAST IS BEST** If it's an option, breast milk is healthier, not only for your baby but also for the environment. It comes without any packaging, and doesn't require fossil-fuel energy to make!

  **MAKE YOUR OWN ORGANIC BABY FOOD** using locally (or home-) grown fruit and vegetables. A batch of pureed fruit and veggies frozen in small containers will last for ages. It will be fresher, cheaper, and tastier than store-bought versions, and is quick and easy to make.

 **LEND, BORROW, AND SWAP BABY EQUIPMENT** Babies grow out of clothes and other equipment at an alarming rate—usually well before they're worn out. Bargains are often available in thrift stores and nearly-new sales and on websites such as Freecycle and eBay.

THE BIG DIAPER DEBATE

Opinions vary about the relative environmental impacts of disposable versus reusable diapers, but both are significant. Whichever you choose, make sure you're minimizing their impact:

- **Reusable diapers** score well on waste, but require a lot of energy for washing, so choose the lowest temperature possible, and avoid using the tumble dryer. Even better, use a diaper-laundering service, which is more efficient than home washing.
- **Disposable diapers** require huge amounts of oil and paper to make and take centuries to decompose in landfill. So if you use disposables, choose a brand that uses materials from sustainable forests; even better, choose biodegradable diapers and have the used ones composted, as they won't break down in landfill.

Studies suggest that about 70% of parents become more **interested in environmental issues** following the birth of their baby.

Babies typically get through more than **5,000 diapers** before they're toilet trained.

Disposable diapers take up to **500 years** to decompose, and it takes a cup of crude oil to produce the plastic for just one diaper—around 8 barrels of oil per child.

In the Netherlands **disposable diapers are composted** in industrial systems and the resulting methane is collected for use as fuel.

Diaper-laundering services use around 30% less energy and 40% less water than home washing.

Using reusable diapers during the first 2½ years of a baby's life generates around **1,250 lb.** of greenhouse gases; using disposables generates about **1,450 lb.**

If every child in America were bottle-fed, almost **95,000 tons of tin plate** would be needed to produce **550 million cans** of formula powder each year.

Use washable baby wipes—either bought or home-made from old material—rather than disposables.

The U.S. toy industry is worth **$22 billion** a year.

!

Americans purchase around **5 billion batteries** each year and produce around 150,000 tons of battery waste annually.

!

Look for toys, such as do-it-yourself solar-power kits and hydrogen model cars, designed to educate and inspire children about **low-carbon technologies**.

✓

The average American child receives **69 new toys** each year.

!

TOYS

Think hard before you buy the latest in-vogue, short-lived plaything for your children; perhaps there's something much simpler that would be more fun for them and less harmful to the planet.

 **BUY SECONDHAND TOYS** Check out eBay, Craigslist, Freecycle, yard sales, or your local classifieds for nearly-new bargains.

 **WOOD'S GOOD** Buy toys made from sustainably grown wood. As a guarantee, look for an FSC (Forest Stewardship Council) logo.

  **JOIN A TOY LIBRARY** to give your children more toys than they could possibly get bored with. Alternatively, **start your own toy-sharing circle** with friends who have children.

 **SPARK YOUR CHILD'S IMAGINATION** by giving them everyday items like cardboard boxes, fabric scraps, shells, or pieces of wood to adapt into their own toys or craft projects, providing hours more fun than manufactured toys.

POWER DOWN

A seemingly unavoidable feature of modern childhood, **electronic toys** are usually made from petrochemical-based plastics. They create significant carbon emissions in their manufacture and produce yet more in their use and disposal. If your child is truly desperate for an electronic toy:

- try to **choose one that's well made** and won't break within weeks
- ideally, **find a toy or game that can be varied or upgraded** (for example, a console that plays a number of different games which can be swapped with friends)
- **invest in a set of rechargeable batteries** and a charger—ideally a solar-powered one
- teach your child(ren) to **switch off the toy** whenever they're not using it.

GOOD HABITS

Avoid scaring your children with apocalyptic horror stories about the daunting challenges facing the planet; instead, help them to understand how to reduce their carbon footprint by teaching them some good habits.

TEAM EFFORT Put your children in charge of some carbon-cutting tasks around the home—for example, checking that lights and appliances are switched off, sorting trash for recycling, or putting suitable waste on a compost pile, if you have one—and reward them for doing well. If you make these chores into enjoyable activities, the habits are likely to last a lifetime.

GET YOUR KIDS GARDENING Encourage them to cultivate some of their favorite fruit and vegetables from scratch—and super-locally. Grow strawberries or tomatoes in pots or sow a patch of salad seeds.

COOKING MASTERCLASS Show your children what to do with their harvest by asking them to help you prepare nutritious meals made

JOIN THE CHAIN GANG

Walking and cycling are both great for avoiding unnecessary carbon emissions, getting your kids fit and healthy, and having fun!

- **Teach a child to ride a bike**. Every 4-mile trip by bike, rather than car, avoids about 2 lb. of CO_2 emissions and builds a strong heart; research shows that regular cyclists tend to be as fit as people 10 years younger who don't do regular exercise.
- If you don't feel confident about you or your children cycling on roads, **enroll in a family cycling proficiency class** to build up your skills and road awareness.
- **Organize family bike rides or walks** during your free time and explore parts of your neighborhood, and pockets of flora and fauna, you'd never know existed if you were sitting in a car.

from fresh ingredients using energy-efficient techniques (see pp.40–42). Instilling in your children the ability to cook will make them less likely to resort to overprocessed prepackaged meals when they've flown the nest.

ASK YOUR CHILD'S SCHOOL FOR BIKE SHELTERS In Denmark 60% of children cycle to school. Encourage your local school to move toward this target by providing secure, covered shelters for pupils and staff.

WALK WAY If your children's school doesn't offer a bus service, resist the temptation to get out the car. Instead, consider joining with other parents to form a "walking bus," taking turns to walk children to school. It's more sociable and reduces the number of cars on the road.

TOYLESS BUT NOT JOYLESS Encourage your children to have fun without toys—plant trees with them, or play simple games like hopscotch or hide and seek. Studies show that children who regularly play in natural environments are healthier, more agile, and better coordinated than their indoor counterparts.

- **Cycle or walk your kids to school.** In 1969, nearly 90% of children aged 5 to 15 who lived within a mile of school traveled there by foot or bicycle. Today, only 31% do so, with many of their classmates covering the short distance by car. With a pepped-up metabolism and fresh air in their lungs, self-propeled children will be fitter and more alert than their car-borne peers. And by staying out of your car, you'll avoid adding to CO_2 emissions and congestion. By switching from the car to a carbon-free journey to school, you'd avoid around 50 lb. of emissions a month for a 2-mile round trip twice a day.

Traffic congestion in the morning rush hour can drop by 30% during **school vacations**.

8

COMPUTERS

Computers may be great inventions, but the modern-day dependence on them is fast becoming an environmental scourge: globally the IT industry accounts for around 2% of CO_2 emissions—about the same as aviation.

CHOOSE A MODEL THAT CAN BE EASILY UPGRADED and so is less likely to become obsolete in the blink of an eye.

MAKE YOUR NEXT COMPUTER A LAPTOP—it will consume up to 90% less energy than a desktop computer.

IF YOU NEED A DESKTOP ... choose one that has a flat LCD (liquid crystal display) screen—they use about 30% less energy than cathode-ray monitors.

SECOND LIFE When they're really no longer useful, give your computer and peripherals to one of the many organizations that now recondition IT equipment for reuse by nonprofit bodies such as schools or charities.

POWER SAVE

Only about 15% of the $250 billion-worth of power used by computers worldwide each year is spent actually computing—the rest is wasted while idling. Use your computer smartly to minimize its electricity consumption:

- **set your computer to enter power-saving mode** after 10 minutes of inactivity—this could cut its energy use by 60–70%
- **shut your computer down** if you're not going to be using it for more than an hour or two—it's a myth that computers use a lot of power to start up
- **don't leave it on overnight**, or you'll waste enough energy to laser print around 800 pages
- **unplug your computer** at the end of the day—it uses a small amount of electricity (about 8 watts) even when fully shut down.

!

It is estimated that an average PC is **in use for 4 hours** each work day and **idle for 5–6 hours**.

✓

If you **upgrade your existing computer**, instead of buying a new one, you could save around 500 lb. of fossil fuel.

✓

Besides saving energy, giving your computer a well-earned rest at the end of each day may **help it to last longer**.

!

Over **31 million** PCs are thrown away worldwide each year.

Screensavers can end up using more energy than not having one, so **switch your screensaver setting to "none" or "blank screen"**.

✓

In U.S. offices, 30–40% of PCs are **left running overnight and at weekends**—using as much energy as 2.5 million cars.

!

The average PC takes around **2 tons** of chemicals, fossil fuels, and water to produce, generates around **220 lb.** of CO_2 per year, and is junked after **3 years**.

!

The plastic alone in each PC system requires nearly **2 gallons of crude oil** to make.

!

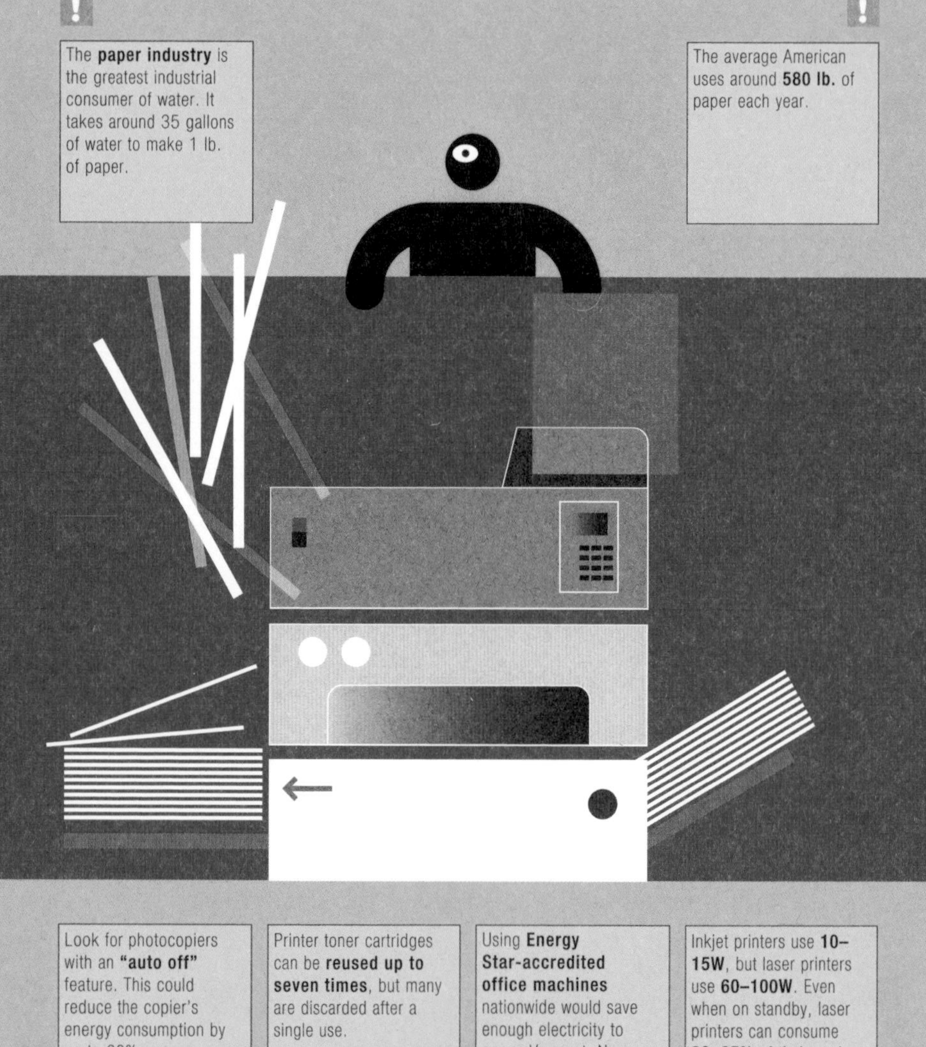

Look for photocopiers with an **"auto off"** feature. This could reduce the copier's energy consumption by up to 60%.

✓

Printer toner cartridges can be **reused up to seven times**, but many are discarded after a single use.

!

Using **Energy Star-accredited office machines** nationwide would save enough electricity to power Vermont, New Hampshire, and Maine.

✓

Inkjet printers use **10–15W**, but laser printers use **60–100W**. Even when on standby, laser printers can consume **30–35%** of their peak power requirements.

!

OFFICE EQUIPMENT & SUPPLIES

Think carefully about how you use the clever equipment filling your office to ensure that your nine-to-five is as efficient and climate-friendly as possible.

SHARE-WARE If your organization shares office space with others, club together to share larger pieces of equipment, such as photocopiers.

IF YOU NEED A NEW PRINTER, BUY A DUPLEX MODEL, which prints on both sides of the paper, halving paper use and reducing energy consumption by around 25%. **Choose an inkjet printer**, if possible, as they use less energy than laser printers. If you need a laser printer, choose one with an energy-saving feature. This reduces energy use when idle by over 65%.

BUY RECYCLED PRINTER CARTRIDGES This will save around a quart of oil per cartridge.

AGAIN AND AGAIN Buy rewritable CDs and DVDs rather than single-use disks—or, even better, save files onto a USB flash drive.

BE A PAPER MISER

Theoretically, many offices are now "paperless," encouraging people to communicate via computer, rather than the printed word. But in reality, paper still represents more than 70% of office waste. So try to get the most out of every scrap:

- **use both sides** of the paper—you'll get through half the volume of wood and other resources used to make it, cutting CO_2 emissions by 2½ lb. for every pound of paper you save
- **buy recycled printer paper and other stationery**—you'll prevent more than 4 lb. of CO_2 emissions with every ream
- before sending a document to print, **run spell check and verify print settings carefully** to minimize wasted printouts
- **read e-mails on screen**—don't print them out unless *really* necessary, and then print only the section you need.

8 CORPORATE ENERGY-SAVING

Don't save all the good work for home—your employer could save huge amounts of energy through company-wide carbon-cutting programs, so do what you can to get the ball rolling.

  **SWITCH OFF LIGHTS AND EQUIPMENT WHEN NOT IN USE** To cut out the human element, install automatic PC shutdown software and movement sensors to make sure lights are in operation only when needed.

  **SMART HEATING AND COOLING** Take a fresh look at the way your company heats and cools its premises, and suggest ways to save energy and money. Don't heat or cool storerooms and corridors unnecessarily, and switch from rigidly seasonal heating to a "smart" program, which reflects the prevailing temperature and is turned down at weekends, at night, and on holidays.

 **LOW-ENERGY COMMUTING** Ask your employer to help workers use less energy for their commute by organizing car-pool programs (see

WHERE DO WE START?

If you're lucky enough to work for an organization with comprehensive environmental policies, make sure you know what they are and contribute to making them work—otherwise they're just another piece of (wasted) paper.

If your company is at a less advanced stage, the first thing it should do is carry out a **carbon audit** to quantify the nature and scale of its impacts. This should look at in-house energy use (by means of energy monitors on different types of equipment and analysis of energy bills) and other CO_2-generating activities such as travel, catering, and ordering office supplies. Specialist footprinting organizations can help with all the carbon counting.

Once your organization knows the nature of the challenge that it faces, it needs to

pp.116–17), encouraging employees to work from home, providing showers and bicycle storage, and gradually reducing parking spaces.

BEAM ME UP Next time you're faced with a long journey to a short meeting, think hard about whether you really need to be there in person. Video conferencing saves money and time, and avoids carbon-heavy travel.

SEND PARCELS BY BIKE Send deliveries around town quickly and cleanly using a bicycle messenger service. Completely carbon-neutral, bikes can nip between jammed traffic, which makes them the swiftest option for urban businesses.

BUY ENERGY-EFFICIENT EQUIPMENT AND APPLIANCES such as computers (see pp.94–5), and make sure they're well maintained.

GIVE YOURSELF A BREAK Governments are increasingly using tax breaks to reward businesses that save energy and levies to penalize energy wasters. Make sure that your organization is fully aware of how it can benefit.

agree on a series of meaningful goals and put together short- and long-term action plans for achieving them. Successful corporate energy-saving programs tend to do the following:

- **clearly communicate** the practical benefits of saving energy, using simple, memorable messages displayed consistently across a variety of media, including posters, company website, and bulletin boards
- **encourage suggestions** from employees of all levels, so that the whole workforce has a strong sense of involvement
- **recognize and reward** employee participation
- **provide regular updates** on progress
- **hold special events**, such as open discussion forums, employee awareness days, and interdepartmental energy-saving competitions.

Lighting an average-sized office overnight wastes enough energy to make **1,000 hot drinks**.

9 SPORTS AND EXERCISE

A burgeoning fitness industry is encouraging us to improve the health of our bodies, but unfortunately much of what's offered isn't so great for the health of the planet. Rethink your exercise routine to trim some carbon pounds.

BUILD EXERCISE INTO YOUR DAILY ROUTINE For example, take the stairs instead of the elevator, carry your recycling to the local depot, and walk, run, or cycle to work or play.

RENT OR BORROW SPORTS EQUIPMENT, unless you use it regularly, to avoid wasting valuable resources on stuff that's only going to collect dust in a closet most of the time.

RECYCLE YOUR RUNNING SHOES The rubber in their soles has a multitude of uses, including all-weather athletic fields.

POOL CARE If you've got a swimming pool, fill it with filtered rainwater, heat it using solar-thermal panels, keep it covered to reduce heat loss, and check it regularly for leaks.

JOIN A GREEN GYM

Instead of driving to an air-conditioned gym to work out on energy-hungry machines, why not **get fit in more natural surroundings**? Get in touch with a local environmental group, and volunteer for carbon-absorbing projects such as tree planting and developing school nature areas.

You can burn up to 30% more calories an hour **creating a nature trail** than doing aerobics.

✓

Cross-country skiing has a lower impact than downhill skiing because it doesn't require chairlifts (or the razing of a mountainside to make way for ski runs).

!

The average **golf course** uses 100 times more water than a four-bedroomed home. Make sure your golf club irrigates sparingly and uses **reclaimed water**.

Covering a swimming pool with an insulating layer can reduce heat loss by as much as 30%.

✓

Ten **gym treadmills** use an average of 13,500kWh of electricity each month—enough to run your hair dryer nonstop **for more than a year**.

!

The hotel chain Marriott runs an **energy-saving program**, which reduces the company's carbon emissions by more than 65,000 tons a year.

Before you go away, remember to **turn off your home heating** (or air-conditioning), or just leave it on a minimum freeze guard setting.

The average hotel guest uses more than **twice the amount of water** they'd normally use at home.

A 100-room hotel could save about 80,000 gallons of water a year through a **linen and towel reuse** program.

Once you've reached your destination, consider **renting bicycles** instead of a car.

HOTELS AND VACATIONS

Keep your vacation's carbon footprint trim by choosing a destination fairly close to home, using low-carbon transportation to reach it, and saving energy once you're there. It's easy to spoil yourself without spoiling the planet.

STAY ON YOUR OWN CONTINENT, and avoid intercontinental long-haul flights, which can produce more CO_2 emissions per passenger than the average motorist does in a year—an easy way of undoing all your good deeds at home. Instead, travel by rail, sea, or road.

SUPPORT LOW-CARBON TRAVEL Contact Sustainable Travel International (www.sustainabletravelinternational.org) to find out how you can help to make the tourism industry greener. You can use their guide to green resorts, make a donation, or become an active member.

EAT LOCAL FOOD ON VACATION The local gastronomic specialties will be fresher and tastier than anything imported and will have caused much less pollution to get to your plate.

LOW-CARBON HOTELS

Make your next hotel stay as energy-efficient as possible:

- **find a hotel with genuine green credentials**—look for one belonging to the Green Tourism Business Scheme or the International Business Leaders Forum Tourism Partnership, or one that's Energy Star-approved
- **turn heating or air-conditioning off**, or at least down, unless it's really necessary, and switch off lights and appliances when they're not needed
- **take showers**, not baths
- **ask to keep the same towels and sheets** for several nights, instead of having them changed daily
- **talk to the manager about the hotel's environmental policies**, and suggest improvements—for example, installing energy-saving lightbulbs, using refillable toiletry containers, or using a renewable energy supply.

CELEBRATIONS

Everyone loves a fantastic party. Next time you're organizing a celebration, make it one to remember by employing some low-carbon party-planning techniques.

 **CELEBRATE EARTH DAY** every April 22.

 **MAKE LOW-IMPACT DECORATIONS**, such as paper chains from magazines or Christmas tree decorations from a stiff dough of flour, water, and a little salt and baked and decorated with colorful trimmings.

 **USE LED CHRISTMAS LIGHTS**, which use up to 95% less energy than traditional bulbs.

  **GIVE LESS "STUFF"** Instead of more potential landfill, give people experiences or services—tickets to an event, a meal out, a certificate for a massage, or a winter's-worth of driveway shoveling. When you do give objects, wrap them in pages from newspapers or magazines, or **use recycled wrapping paper tied with ribbons**, so the paper can be used again.

TYING THE KNOT

Make your special day really special by minimizing its environmental impact:

- **source local products**—particularly food, drink, and flowers
- **rent linens, furniture, glasses**, and so on, rather than buying them
- **look for organic or recycled outfits** for a unique, low-impact look
- avoid supporting the energy-intensive mining of heavy metals by **choosing antique rings**
- **select an easily accessible venue**, and encourage your guests to travel there by low-carbon forms of transportation
- **give guests each a low-energy lightbulb** as a wedding favor
- **ask for gifts that will help support your low-carbon life** together, such as his and hers bikes, fruit trees, or public transportation passes. Or **set up an online donation registry** to a charity running low-carbon projects.

✓

Send seasonal greetings by e-mail to cut down on the amount of extra paper being mailed around the globe.

The average American **wedding** has 165 guests, of which 54 travel to the ceremony by air.

!

A typical string of **Christmas tree lights** left on for 10 hours a day over the Christmas period produces enough CO_2 to fill 50 party balloons.

!

In 2006, 189 million roses were grown for **Valentine's Day** in the U.S.

!

The ingredients for a typical **Christmas dinner** travel up to 30,000 miles.

!

Almost **7 million walking journeys** are made in **London** every day, and walking accounts for 80% of all trips under 1 mile.

Cycling for half an hour a day can increase life expectancy by up to **4 years**.

It costs an average of **$4,000 a year to run a car** in the U.S., taking into account factors such as fuel cost, insurance, and maintenance.

!

The League of American Bicyclists awards **Bicycle-Friendly Community** status to U.S. municipalities that actively support cycling.

In **Copenhagen, Denmark** (which is ranked one of the happiest countries in the world), **36% of commuters travel by bicycle**.

Replace a 5-mile car trip with a bike ride once a week. This will prevent around 200 lb. of CO_2 emissions a year: equivalent to watching TV solidly for 75 days.

In Manhattan, **82%** of residents commute by walking, cycling, or public transportation—and produce **less than a third** of the CO_2 of an average American.

USING YOUR LEGS

Over half the oil extracted worldwide is used for transportation, a major cause of CO_2 emissions. To slow down the burn, use your legs to walk or cycle wherever and whenever you can. You'll benefit the health of both yourself and the planet.

WALK 10,000 STEPS A DAY (around 4–5 miles), as recommended by health experts, using a pedometer to measure your progress.

EQUIP YOUR BIKE FOR CARGO Buy a basket for the front of your bicycle and some strong panniers for the back.

SHARE A BIKE Use city bike-hire programs such as Vélib' in Paris, Call-a-Bike in Germany, and OYBike in Britain. Ask your local government for a similar program if there isn't one in your area.

FOLLOW THE TRAIL Ask your national cycling association for a map of local cycle routes.

GET A JOB CLOSE TO HOME, so you can walk or cycle to work for a carbon-free commute.

A DECONGESTANT THAT WORKS!

Congestion charging, a system involving charging drivers a fee to enter a designated zone during peak periods, has been a real success story in cities such as London, Singapore, and Stockholm. In London, for example, the congestion charge has encouraged 500,000 drivers a day to leave their cars at home and travel into the city center by foot, bicycle, or public transportation. Carbon emissions are down 16%, traffic delays have been cut by over 20%, and the local economy is thriving. Such strategies generate significant revenue to invest in public transportation and walking and cycling programs. In 2007 the mayor of New York announced plans to introduce congestion charging for the busiest parts of Manhattan. Why not **lobby your local government to consider congestion charging** for your home town?

PUBLIC TRANS-PORTATION

If your trip's too long, you've got too much to carry, or the weather's too awful to walk or cycle, using public transportation is a lower-carbon way of getting around than driving your car.

CELEBRATE WORLD CAR-FREE DAY, which is held each year on September 22, by leaving your car at home for 24 hours. If you normally commute by car, use this day to **try out an alternative way to get to work**. Taking the bus for a 15-mile round trip to work each day could cut your carbon footprint by nearly 1.5 tons of CO_2 per year.

ADJUST YOUR WORKING HOURS, if you can, so that you don't have to travel on public transportation at peak times. The journey will be quicker, and you'll be guaranteed a seat.

GET A MULTIPURPOSE TRAVEL CARD, if they're available where you live, so you can take advantage of public transportation as the mood strikes you and always get the best deal.

PASSENGER MPG

The true fuel efficiency of a vehicle depends on the number of passengers it's carrying, a figure expressed in terms of "passenger miles per gallon" (vehicle mpg multiplied by number of passengers). So, for example, the typical car averaging 30mpg and carrying two passengers is doing **60pmpg**, whereas a bus that averages 6mpg while carrying 40 passengers is doing **240pmpg**—four times as efficient as the car.

The French **TGV** high-speed train can travel at an average speed of more than **150mph**.

✓

The Bogotá (Colombia) rapid transit system carries **1,600** passengers per bus per day and has achieved a **32%** reduction in journey time and a **40%** reduction in greenhouse emissions.

!

Carbon **emissions per passenger** per 1,000 miles vary greatly:
Bus—270 lb.;
Train—450 lb.;
Small car—590 lb.;
Airplane—970 lb.;
SUV—1,570 lb.

✓

Ask your government to support public transportation by increasing the cost of driving private cars and using the revenue to **fund improved public transportation**.

✓

Public transportation generates **95% less** carbon monoxide and **50% less** carbon dioxide and nitrogen oxide per passenger mile than private cars.

✓

If all car drivers switched to public transportation, CO_2 emissions from transportation would be reduced by **90%**.

!

Drivers in America's most congested cities spend more than **40 hours** a year (an entire working week) sitting in stationary traffic.

JUMP ON A LOCAL BUS and you'll help to empty the roads. A bus can carry the occupants of 20 cars, producing far less pollution and taking up far less space on the road.

TAKE THE TRAIN, a great way to travel long distances with minimal environmental impact. Unlike flying, you don't have to waste time checking in hours before departure, and, unlike driving, you can get stuff done en route—even if only catching up on some sleep!

SAVE A BUSLOAD OF CARBON Traveling long distance by bus is an even lower carbon option than train travel—switching from car to bus can cut the CO_2 produced by your journey by up to 90%.

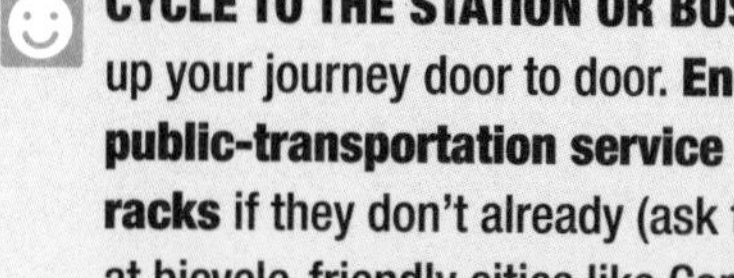

CYCLE TO THE STATION OR BUS STOP to speed up your journey door to door. **Encourage your public-transportation service to provide bike racks** if they don't already (ask them to look at bicycle-friendly cities like Copenhagen for inspiration), or **buy a folding bicycle**, which you can take on board and then unfold for a quick getaway at the other end.

BREAKING THE CHAIN

The shape of the modern developed world has been heavily influenced by the automobile. Out-of-town shopping malls and supermarkets, designed to be reached by car, are supplanting the traditional downtown shopping districts, so that, even with the best intentions, it's hard not to drive on a regular basis.

It'll be a hard trend to reverse, but designing communities with stores and amenities within walking or cycling distance and well served by public transportation is key to making low-carbon living a reality. Cities worldwide are taking up the challenge in different ways. Bogotá, in Colombia, and Curitiba, in Brazil, have bus rapid transit systems with exclusive routes for buses (the inspiration for the recently opened Los Angeles Orange Line), and many cities, including London and Stockholm, are using congestion charging (see p.107) as a means of getting people out of their cars and onto public transportation.

ECO-DRIVING

Road traffic generates a large—and growing—proportion of man-made CO_2 emissions. The way in which we maintain and drive our cars has a huge impact on fuel efficiency.

SLOW DOWN! Faster driving uses more fuel, so try to exert gentle pressure on the accelerator and keep speeds down to maximize your mpg.

AVOID EXCESS WEIGHT OR DRAG—it costs you fuel. Leave the luggage rack behind, and take heavy items (golf clubs, etc.) out of the trunk if you're not using them. Carrying an extra 100 lb. can reduce fuel efficiency by nearly 2%.

GET YOUR CAR SERVICED REGULARLY This should pay for itself in saved fuel. An inefficient, poorly maintained engine can reduce your car's fuel efficiency by 10% or more.

USE THE RIGHT GEAR If you've got a gearshift car, move up to top gear as soon as possible without accelerating harder than necessary. However, **don't let the engine labor** in a high

THINK BEFORE YOU DRIVE

Journeys of less than two miles cause the most pollution per mile: a straining cold engine produces 60% more emissions than a warm one. So, before you jump in the car, **ask yourself whether you really need to drive**. If you can, time your car journeys to **avoid rush hour**—sitting in traffic, your fuel efficiency goes down to zero mpg. **Combine various errands into a single trip** and you'll save time, effort, and money.

Driving at **50mph** uses **30% less fuel** than driving at **70mph**.

gear when traveling uphill, as this will use more fuel and put stress on the engine. If you've got an automatic, ease back slightly on the accelerator as the car gathers momentum, so that the transmission can shift up quickly and smoothly.

SMOOTHLY DOES IT Studies have shown that an aggressive driving style characterized by sharp acceleration, high speeds, and hard braking reduces travel time by only 4% on average, while increasing fuel consumption by up to 40%. Avoid unnecessarily marked changes of speed by keeping your distance from the vehicle in front, slowing down gradually when approaching junctions and red lights, and keeping passing to a minimum. **Try driving in soft-soled shoes**—this should help you to really feel the pedals.

LAY OFF THE A/C, because using it can increase fuel consumption by more than 20% in city driving. Unless it's stiflingly hot, **roll down the windows** instead. If you're traveling faster than 45mph, it's more efficient to **use your car's flow-through ventilation** than to roll down the windows, because at higher speeds open windows increase the drag on the car.

CHECK IT OUT!

Besides sticking to a regular professional car servicing and tuning schedule, there are a number of key maintenance tasks you can undertake yourself to improve your car's fuel performance:

- **Maintain the correct tire pressures**—ideally, check your tires every week or two. Driving with underinflated tires increases resistance against the road surface, which makes the engine work harder and use more fuel. It will also increase the rate of tire wear and affect the car's handling.
- **Check your oil level**, and use the recommended grade of oil. A well-lubricated engine uses less fuel.
- **Look out for oil leaks**, and get them fixed immediately.
- **Replace clogged air filters**, which reduce engine efficiency. In regions of above-average pollution, filters may become blocked more quickly.

For every **6,000 miles** the average car travels, it generates **its own weight in CO_2** emissions.

A car traveling at **40mph in fifth gear** uses around **25% less fuel** than one traveling at the same speed in **third gear**.

There were just over **600 million private cars** on the world's roads **in 2007**; it's predicted there'll be up to **2.7 billion by 2050**.

Every **gallon of gasoline** saved keeps **20 lb. of CO_2** out of the atmosphere—so every increase in fuel efficiency makes a difference!

When just **1% of car owners properly maintain** their vehicles, more than **400,000 tons of CO_2** is kept out of the atmosphere.

In the Netherlands, **eco-driving forms part of the driving test**.

✓

Skipping just **one 5-hour flight** could cut your CO_2 emissions by a ton, equivalent to **160 days of commuting** 10 miles each way in a medium-size car.

!

With proportionally more fuel used for takeoff, the carbon footprint per passenger mile for **short-haul** flights is up to 25% larger than for **long-haul** flights.

!

At this very moment, there are around **12,000** civil aircraft in the sky.

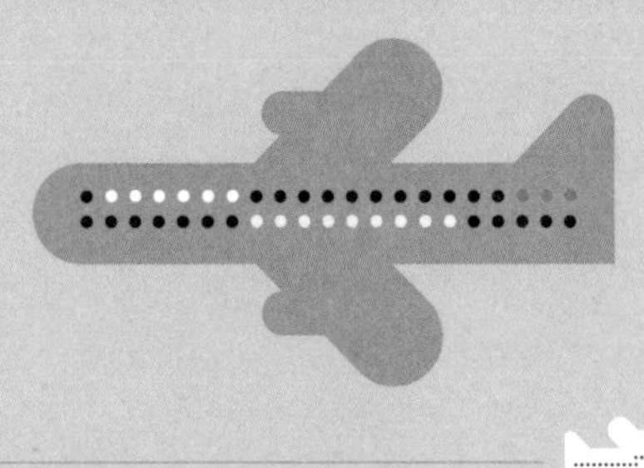

Air passengers carried (worldwide):

1985	0.9 billion
2005	2 billion
2025	4.5 billion (forecast)

North America accounts for **40%** of worldwide air traffic.

!

Taking the train instead of flying on a round trip from New York to Boston produces around 150 lb. less CO_2 per passenger.

✓

A plane uses about as much fuel, and therefore produces about as much CO_2, as would **every passenger on board driving their own car** the same distance.

!

One round-trip flight from New York to San Francisco would wipe out the CO_2 savings made by running a hybrid car (see p.120) for a year.

!

FLIGHT-FREE TRIPS

It's a tough one to swallow, but cutting out non-essential flights is probably the single most important thing you can do to reduce your carbon footprint.

EMBRACE THE ART OF SLOW TRAVEL, and treat the journey as part of the experience. Enjoy avoiding the hassles of security checks, in-flight inedibles, and baggage reclaim; on journeys of several hundred miles you'll probably find flight-free travel's quicker anyway! **Plan flight-free trips worldwide** using the independent Man in Seat 61 website (www.seat61.com).

GO BY RAIL On average, trains emit two-thirds less CO_2 per passenger than planes.

TRAVEL ON A CARGO SHIP You'll save money, visit places the average tourist never sees, and dramatically slash your journey's carbon emissions. Or join the crew of a sailing boat for an invigorating, zero-carbon tour of the seas. But **avoid large cruise liners**, which are laden with energy-guzzling extravagances.

WHY IS FLYING BAD FOR THE PLANET?

Besides releasing 3–4% of man-made CO_2 emissions, aviation contributes to climate change in other significant ways—for example, by emitting nitrogen oxides, which form the greenhouse gas ozone. And because this happens at high altitude, the impact is magnified. Taken as a whole, **the warming effect of air travel is calculated to be 2.7 times greater than that of its CO_2 emissions alone**, meaning that it accounts for around 10% of overall man-made climate emissions. What makes things worse is that **aviation is the fastest-growing source of man-made emissions**, growing by around 5% a year, far outstripping any efficiencies that can be achieved through improved technology. If it continues to grow at this rate, we'd have to eliminate emissions from almost all other sources to have a chance of achieving the reductions required to limit climate change to 2°C.

10 CAR-SHARING

Try car-pooling or joining a city car-share instead of owning your own four wheels. You'll save money and hassle and cut your carbon footprint considerably.

NEIGHBORLY SHARING If you get along with your neighbors, try jointly owning and maintaining a car.

SHARE A LIFT TO WORK If everyone who regularly drives to work on their own shared a lift just once a week, traffic volumes would fall by 12–15%.

START A CAR-POOL with friends or coworkers. Organize it yourself, or **use a specialist website** to link up with people doing similar journeys.

JOIN A CAR-SHARE PROGRAM These operate in many cities, providing self-service, pay-as-you-go cars. You reserve a car by phone or via the Internet, use it for as long as you need, paying by the hour and/or mile, then leave it in a designated parking bay for the next user.

LEADING BY EXAMPLE

Companies can do much to reduce the carbon footprint of their employees' journeys to and from work. Why not suggest the following strategies to your employer:

- **run a car-pool** via the company intranet or a central bulletin board
- **trade in the company car fleet** for a corporate membership of a car-share program
- **offer incentives** for green commuting, such as an extra day of annual leave.

Members of car-share programs drive **47% fewer miles** each year than car owners.

!

The average moving car in the U.S. contains only **1.5 people**.

✓

The average Western commuter burns **340 gallons** of fuel a year, creating a **3¾-ton** cloud of CO_2. Joining a car-pool can cut that figure by half or more.

✓

There are car-share programs running in more than **600 cities** worldwide.

!

Every **1,000 miles** you travel in an average-size gas-fueled family sedan that does 35mpg causes **600–700 lb.** of CO_2 emissions.

If you drive less than 7,500 miles a year and don't need a car for work every day, joining a **car-share program** will save you thousands of dollars a year.

✓

The average American spends **18 cents of every dollar** they earn on buying, running, and maintaining cars.

!

In North America, **priority lanes** for vehicles occupied by two people or more are a common way to incentivize car-pooling.

✓

It takes **79 tons of plant material** and **10 million years** to produce one gallon of gasoline.

The manure from America's **8.5 million dairy cows** could be used to generate enough **biomethane** to power **a million cars**.

To power all the vehicles on the world's roads with **biofuel** would require **five to six times** more land than is currently used for growing crops.

Worldwide, there are currently **11 million LPG-fueled vehicles**.

Sweden has a fleet of **8,000 biomethane-powered** buses and garbage trucks. In 2006, it agreed to share its expertise with the state of California.

Brazil, the world leader in **bioethanol** production, accounted for **37% of the 11 billion gallons** produced in 2004.

Hydrogen fuel cells could be the long-term answer if a sustainable method of sourcing the hydrogen (currently produced by burning gas) can be found.

The U.S. generates more than **2½ billion gallons of waste vegetable oil** each year—equivalent to 1% of total national oil demand.

FUEL TYPES

As fossil-fuel supplies diminish, and as the problems of climate change escalate, the race to find low-carbon alternatives is on. As yet, there is no clear winner.

CHOOSE DIESEL OVER GASOLINE Diesel engines are more fuel efficient and produce up to 40% less CO_2 than their gas equivalents. However, they emit more nitrogen oxide and particulate pollution, so if you're buying a diesel car, **make sure it has a particulate filter**.

GREASED LIGHTNING If you have an old diesel car, have it converted to run on waste vegetable oil from food factories and fast-food restaurants.

CONVERT YOUR CAR TO RUN ON LPG (liquefied petroleum gas). Widely available, it produces about as much CO_2 as diesel does, but much less nitrogen oxide and particulate pollution. Another option for some is **compressed natural gas**. Even cleaner than LPG, it's popular in countries such as Italy, India, and Argentina, but not yet available worldwide.

BIOFUELS

Practically anything organic can be transformed into biofuels such as **biodiesel** and **bioethanol**. When made from renewable sources, such as vegetable oil, these fuels are theoretically carbon neutral, since the CO_2 they emit is absorbed in new plant growth. The drawback is that there simply isn't enough land to grow sufficient biofuels to meet a significant proportion of the demand without seriously affecting food production.

Biomethane gas produced from materials such as sewage, silage, and kitchen waste is a promising biofuel option. It produces less CO_2 and other emissions than any other fuel. However, a whole new infrastructure of biomethane refueling stations would be needed if biomethane were to replace gas or diesel on a significant scale. But it has huge potential as a fuel for public transportation systems, car fleets, and agricultural vehicles.

CARS

When buying a new car, make sure that it's better for the environment than the last one. (And ask yourself whether you need a car at all ...)

CHOOSE THE SMALLEST CAR AND ENGINE that will meet your everyday needs. Look for the car with the lowest emissions in your chosen category, and save money on both fuel and tax.

BUY AN ELECTRIC CAR If you charge it from a renewable electricity supply (see p.13), it will produce 97% fewer emissions than a gas-powered counterpart. Small electric cars average the equivalent of 600mpg, but their battery technology limits their range to around 50 miles.

BEST OF BOTH WORLDS Try a hybrid car for a balance between efficiency and range. Hybrids are powered by an electric battery at low speeds and gas at higher speeds. The battery is recharged using the kinetic energy produced when you apply the brakes or travel downhill.

THE LEAST BAD OPTION

Strictly speaking, there's no such thing as a "green car"—even the most efficient model takes a great deal of resources and energy to make and requires an environmentally damaging infrastructure of roads and parking lots. The Norwegian government feels so strongly about this that they've banned advertisements that focus on cars' green credentials, pointing out that **"cars cannot do anything good for the environment except less damage than others."**

Whatever car you choose, make a pledge to **use it less** and **share it more!**

Choose a model with manual transmission. If you follow the principles of eco-driving (see pp.111–13), manual models tend to be more fuel-efficient than automatics.

Minimize add-ons such as global-positioning systems—they can add to your car's weight and/or sap its battery, both of which lead to reduced fuel efficiency.

You can save **a ton of CO_2** every year if your new car is just **2mpg more efficient** than your current one.

A **stop-start system**, which switches off your car's engine whenever you stop and uses electricity from the battery to move forward again, can **increase mpg by up to 15%**.

Large **SUVs** take 50% more energy to manufacture and produce around 80% more CO_2 per mile than the average car.

Hybrid and electric cars **attract income tax breaks** in the U.S. and are **exempt from the congestion charge** in London (see p.107).

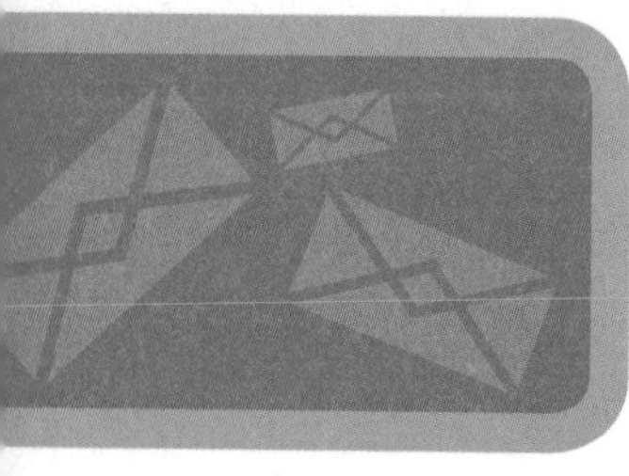

THE BIGGER PICTURE

There's undoubtedly a lot we can each do to reduce our own carbon footprint. But to achieve the scale of change required at the pace necessary to avoid the worst impacts of climate change will demand action at all levels of society.

WRITE TO YOUR ELECTED REPRESENTATIVE to express your support for legislative change that speeds up the transition to a low-carbon society.

VOTE for the party with the strongest commitment to tackling climate change.

GET LOCALLY ACTIVE Petition for change in your local government, and get involved in one of the environmental groups in your area.

CONVINCE A SKEPTIC Fighting to reduce your own carbon footprint is good; persuading others to do the same is even better.

JOIN A NONGOVERNMENTAL ORGANIZATION (NGO) that's campaigning for action to address climate change.

SUPPORT LOW-CARBON COMMUNITIES

Take inspiration from the many places around the world that are already moving toward low-carbon living. For example:

- **Boulder**, Colorado, which has recently approved America's first "climate tax"
- **Ashton Hayes** in rural Cheshire, which is aiming to become Britain's first "carbon-neutral village"
- the growing network of **"transition towns"** such as Totnes in Devon, England, which are actively trying to break their fossil-fuel dependency
- **Stockholm**, Sweden, which is planning to become fossil fuel-free by 2050, with initiatives including biofuel-powered heating, renewably-fueled buses and biogas-powered municipal vehicles
- the **450+ U.S. cities** (inhabited by more than 62 million people) whose mayors have signed a Climate Protection Agreement to reduce emissions.

Rising seas will put an estimated **70 million** African lives at risk of flooding by 2080, displacing the people least responsible for climate change.

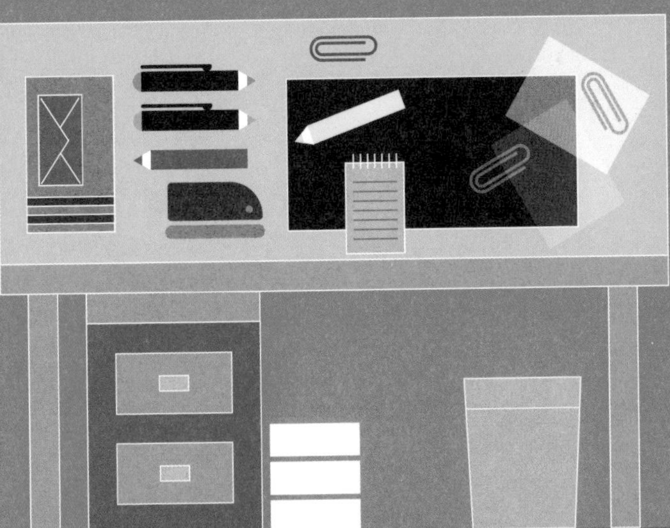

Align your finances. Consider moving any investments you have—including your mortgage—to a fund that supports action on climate change.

Recognizing that **cities generate 80% of CO_2 emissions**, the world's largest cities have formed a group called **C40** to tackle climate change.

A heartening **81% of U.S. citizens** agree with the statement "It is my responsibility to help reduce the impacts of global warming."

New **investments in renewable energy** could create 3.3 million jobs worldwide in the next 10 years.

FURTHER READING AND USEFUL WEBSITES

FURTHER READING

Chris Goodall, *How to Live a Low Carbon Life.* Earthscan, 2007

Al Gore, *An Inconvenient Truth.* Rodale, 2006

Robert Henson, *The Rough Guide to Climate Change.* Rough Guides, 2006

Mark Lynas, *Carbon Counter.* Collins Gem, 2007

George Monbiot, *Heat.* South End Press, 2007

David de Rothschild, *The Live Earth Global Warming Survival Handbook.* Rodale, 2007

Nicky Scott, *Composting.* Green Books, 2006.

Godo Stoyke, *The Carbon Buster's Home Energy Handbook.* New Society, 2007

Various authors, *Recycle: The Essential Guide.* Black Dog Publishing, 2006

Worldwatch Institute, *Vital Signs: The Trends that are Shaping our Future.* Norton, published annually

USEFUL WEBSITES

General information and advice

EarthCorps (www.earthcorps.org)—a practical environmental charity that helps people to make positive changes at home, at work, at school, and in the wider community

Earthwatch Institute (www.earthwatch.org)

The Ecologist online magazine (www.theecologist.org)

Friends of the Earth (www.foe.org)

Greenpeace USA (www.greenpeace.org/usa/)

Ideal Bite (www.idealbite.com)—daily green living tips

Live Earth (www.liveearth.org)—following on from the Live Earth concerts in July 2007, a great online tool providing information on climate change and reducing carbon emissions

Treehugger (www.treehugger.com)—in-depth blog-style website about green lifestyles

Worldwatch Institute (www.worldwatch.org)—a leading source of information on the interactions among key environmental, social, and economic trends

Carbon footprint calculators

Carbon Footprint (www.carbonfootprint.com)

Earthlab (www.earthlab.com/carbonProfile/LiveEarth.htm?ver=14)

Environmental Protection Agency (www.epa.gov/climatechange/emissions/ind_calculator.html)

Children

Green Schools Association (Alliance to Save Energy) (www.ase.org/section/program/greenschl)

National Association of Diaper Services (www.diapernet.org)

U.S. Toy Library Association (www.usatla.home.comcast.net)

Waste Free Lunches (www.wastefreelunches.org)

Energy-saving advice and products

Eco Business Links (www.ecobusinesslinks.com)—source of green, natural, and ethical businesses and organizations

Eco Mall (www.ecomall.com)

Energy Star (www.energystar.gov)—government program to promote energy-efficient products and practices

Rocky Mountain Institute (www.rmi.org)

Savawatt (www.savawatt.com)

WattStopper (www.wattstopper.com)

Food and drink

American Vegan Society (www.americanvegan.org)

The Ecological Farming Association (www.eco-farm.org)—promotes sustainable, organic farming

International Vegetarian Union (www.ivu.org)

Local Harvest (www.localharvest.org)—find farmers' markets and CSA programs in your area

Renewable energy suppliers

The Green Power Network (www.eere.energy.gov/greenpower/)—find a green electricity supplier

Shopping

Buy Nothing Day (www.adbusters.org/metas/eco/bnd/)

Craigslist (www.craigslist.org)—classified listings

Freecycle (www.freecycle.org)—nonprofit network for giving and receiving unwanted property for free

Travel and transport

Green Hotels Association (www.greenhotels.com)

Institute for Transportation and Development Policy (www.itdp.org)

League of American Bicyclists (www.bikeleague.org)

The National Coalition of Walking Advocates (www.americawalks.org)

Waste

National Recycling Program (www.nrc-recycle.org)

Zero Waste America (www.zerowasteamerica.org)

INDEX